D0036577

Walking on Water

When You Feel Like

You're Drowning

WALKING
ON WATER
when you feel like you're drowning

FINDING HOPE IN LIFE'S DARKEST MOMENTS

TOMMY NELSON
STEVE LEAVITT

Tyndale House Publishers, Inc. • Carol Stream, Illinois

Walking on Water When You Feel Like You're Drowning
Copyright © 2012 by Tommy Nelson and Steve Leavitt
All rights reserved

A Focus on the Family book published by Tyndale House Publishers, Inc., Carol Stream, Illinois 60188

Focus on the Family and the accompanying logo and design are federally registered trademarks of Focus on the Family, Colorado Springs, CO 80995.

TYNDALE and Tyndale's quill logo are registered trademarks of Tyndale House Publishers, Inc.

Unless otherwise noted, Scripture taken from the New King James Version®. Copyright © 1982 by Thomas Nelson, Inc. Used by permission. All rights reserved.

Scripture quotations marked (NIV) are taken from the Holy Bible, New International Version®, NIV®. Copyright © 1973, 1978, 1984 by Biblica, Inc.™ Used by permission of Zondervan. All rights reserved worldwide. www.zondervan.com. The "NIV" and "New International Version" are trademarks registered in the United States Patent and Trademark Office by Biblica, Inc.™ Scripture quotations marked (NASB) taken from the New American Standard Bible®, copyright © 1960, 1962, 1963, 1968, 1971, 1972, 1973, 1975, 1977, 1995 by The Lockman Foundation. Used by permission. (www.Lockman.org)

No part of this publication may be reproduced, stored in a retrieval system, or transmitted in any form or by any means—electronic, mechanical, photocopy, recording, or otherwise—without prior written permission of Focus on the Family.

Editor: Ray Seldomridge

Cover design by Ron Kaufmann

Cover photograph copyright © Karen Kasmauski/National Geographic Society/Corbis. All rights reserved.

For information about special discounts for bulk purchases, please contact Tyndale House Publishers at csresponse@tyndale.com, or call 1-800-323-9400.

Cataloging-in-Publication Data for this book is available by contacting the Library of Congress at http://www.loc.gov/help/contact-general.html.

ISBN: 978-1-58997-722-8

Printed in the United States of America

23 22 21 20 19 18 17
10   9   8   7   6   5   4

TOMMY

To my wife, Teresa, who walked with me
through the darkest part of my life
To my family, who kept me laughing in the saddest time of my life
To the saints of Denton Bible Church,
who encouraged me in the toughest part of my life
And to God, who—by His sustaining grace—walked with me
in the "valley of the shadow"

STEVE

To my amazing wife, Marty, who loves me beyond measure,
often when I don't deserve it
To Tommy Nelson, who has poured so much into me over the years
To Buddy Vaughn, without whom this book
would have never happened

CONTENTS

Introduction—Roaring Wind and Rising Waves 1

PART ONE: The Dark Descent

1 That Sinking Feeling 9
How the trouble began

2 Deeper & Deeper 21
Anxiety, obsessions, fear . . . and Scripture

3 Sunk! 33
Trials, tribulations, suffering . . . and Scripture

PART TWO: Questions from the Depths of Despair

4 How Did I Get Here? 45
Identifying the source of your depression

5 Who Else Has Been Here? 61
A noble company of the anxious and obsessed

6 What's Going On in My Mind? 75
I can't stop obsessing about it!

7 What's Going On in My Body? 83
I feel like I am dying!

8 What's Going On in My Spirit?. 93
    Deciding who is in control

PART THREE: Keys to Recovery

9 Escape the Performance Trap. 103
    Avoiding the poison of perfectionism

10 Change Your Mind 111
    Stop believing the lies

11 Get Help from Loved Ones. 119
    How to involve others in your healing

12 Set Boundaries. 127
    When to say, "It's not gonna happen!"

13 Let Medications Help 131
    Where drugs fit in for a Christian

14 Live for the Long Haul 143
    Taking preventive measures

Final Thoughts—Walking on Water 151
    Seven steps to joy, rest, contentment, and hope

ABOUT THE AUTHORS

Tommy Nelson

Tommy Nelson has served at Denton Bible Church (Denton, Texas) for thirty-five years, much of that time as senior pastor. One of four boys, he comes from Waco, Texas, and grew up playing football and baseball. He holds degrees from the University of North Texas (where he quarterbacked) and Dallas Theological Seminary. Tommy has written several books, teaches on DVDs, and is the Song of Solomon Conference Speaker Emeritus. He is a featured speaker for several national ministries.

Tommy married his best friend, Teresa, in 1972. Their two sons, Benjamin and John Clark, are both married and have given them six grandchildren.

Steve Leavitt

Steve Leavitt is a Christian biblical counselor in New Braunfels, Texas. He graduated from Dallas Theological Seminary with a master of arts in biblical counseling. An ordained minister who has been ministering and counseling for over twenty-five years, Steve has an extensive teaching ministry through speaking and CDs on the subjects of marriage, parenting, and biblical solutions to anxiety and depression. For more information, see www.hopeforlifeministry.com or call 866-999-HOPE (4673).

Steve has a wonderful wife, Marty, and four children ages 9–16.

Roaring Wind and Rising Waves

Tommy

Football was my sole obsession from adolescence through college. I spent every waking moment reading about it, watching it, practicing, or conditioning for my role as a quarterback. It was a blessing to be "slightly better than average," because I learned that while many players had more talent than I did, I could nonetheless outwork them. Intensity became my coin of the realm.

The focus of my life changed in 1972 when I came to Jesus Christ and received Him as my Savior and Lord. The Word of God, prayer, sharing the faith, memorizing Scripture, discipling other men, preaching and teaching—these were all more than worthy of a life of devotion.

Between 1974 and 1976, my wife, Teresa, and I began with 15 collegians at a Methodist church and grew to a group of 160. We helped start Denton Bible Church in Denton, Texas, and saw it grow from

100 to 4,000 plus. I also wrote several books and helped a singles study group in Dallas grow from 200 to 2,000 in seven years.

As if that weren't enough to keep me busy, I joined a friend and fellow minister, Doug Hudson, in his endeavor to teach the Song of Solomon to large conferences all over the nation. And I began my own program called Young Guns, in which I would take thirty to fifty college graduates a year and teach them four mornings a week on numerous books of Scripture. More than 600 men went through the program from 1990 to 2006, with at least 100 later enrolling in Dallas Seminary.

The impact of Denton Bible's ministry over those sixteen years was incredible. But its toll on me was heavy. Preaching and teaching from morning till night, day in and day out, was clearly stressful. However, since I enjoyed what I was doing, I didn't see any problem. By faith, I could handle the wind and the waves, no matter how rough, and still walk tall.

I never thought you could burn out doing what you loved. I was wrong.

Other events compounded the stress associated with overextending myself. I was ministering to my wife at a low time in her life after she had taken care of her dying father. Moreover, my own mother had gone through two major surgeries. And my church had just built a twenty-million-dollar sanctuary and learning center with all the organizational and financial burdens that went with it.

But the thing is that I loved every second. No one *made* me disciple men; I did it because I longed to put the Word of God in their hearts and watch the light come on in their understanding. I also enjoyed the fulfillment and satisfaction of contributing to others' lives.

I even had projects lined up for the future. I'd planned a conference in which to teach the book of Romans in twelve taped sessions to 800 folks. I was also scheduled to teach in New York, in North Carolina, and at the Mount Hermon Conference Center in California. Beyond that, I sought to put the Young Guns program on video so I could start programs around the country, where more and more men would learn the Scriptures from the same source.

So many times, I would awaken in the night and check the clock, hoping it was almost time to get up and go at it again. My wife repeatedly warned me about overworking, but I simply ran past the warning signs she was flashing. I never thought you could burn out doing what you loved. I was wrong.

Steve

Since you're reading this book, you or someone you love is probably emotionally distressed. That's why Tommy and I are going to take a biblical look at stress, fear, worry, anxiety, panic attacks, perfectionism, obsessiveness, and depression.

Though emotional stresses stem from a variety of causes and experiences, they all have at least one thing in common: We don't think rightly about our circumstances. The way we think makes an incredible difference. So one of the most important tools we can use in our recovery is to get rid of our "stinkin' thinkin'." When that cycle is broken, and we've dealt with other contributing factors as well, we can begin to find the relief and peace we're searching for.

Let me put it another way. We do what we do because we believe what we believe. If you change what you perceive to be true, you will change the way you live.

Scripture says that Satan is the "father of lies," and he desires to destroy us. But God is the God of truth, and He tells us that the truth will set us free. So we're going to expose the lies that Satan continues to use.

Once a middle-aged man sat on my counseling couch and said, "It's hopeless. There is no way to ever stop feeling the way I feel." This gentleman had made lots of money, raised wonderful kids, enjoyed a great marriage, and served God for twenty years. Suddenly his world had crashed around him, and he realized he was not in control of anything, which was terribly disconcerting for him. He needed *truth* to be set free—the truth that God was in control. Just because the man *felt* hopeless didn't mean that life really *was* hopeless. But the lie he had believed was killing him.

Consider this book to be your emotional tool chest. It's going to give you all the tools you need for the problems you face on the journey toward healing. Whether you're wrestling with depression or obsessive-compulsive thinking, or you are just full of anxiety and fear, this book will help.

As you start the journey, one of the first things you may wonder is whether there really is any basis for hope. By God's power and grace, absolutely! So, what have you hoped in that has let you down?

Your spouse?

Your children not being who you want them to be?

Your friends?

A stressful job (or no job)?

Your finances?

Your health?

Your God?

I recently visited with a woman who felt hopeless and was just minutes away from taking her own life. She was both outwardly and inwardly beautiful. She had wonderful children, a loving husband, financial security, and loved God with all her heart, but she still felt desperately hopeless.

Through the grace of God, medication, and biblical counseling, she is now hopeful and looking forward to what God has planned. Her story has been repeated hundreds of times in my twenty years of counseling and is foundational to what we are talking about, because we serve a God of hope.

What have you hoped in that has let you down?

Yahweh (the one true God) is a God you can hope in and a God you can trust. If you are suffering today or know someone who is, take comfort from the Word of God. God has revealed himself to us and longs to give us hope that is centered on the truth of who He is. Have hope in the One who sent His Son to redeem you.

> Remember your word to your servant,
>> for you have given me hope. (Psalm 119:49, NIV)

> The righteous cry out, and the LORD hears them;
>> he delivers them from all their troubles.
> The LORD is close to the brokenhearted
>> and saves those who are crushed in spirit. (Psalm 34:17–18, NIV)

the dark descent

ONE

That Sinking Feeling

How the trouble began

Tommy

Back in 1992, a friend of mine dared me to teach the Song of Solomon—the Bible's celebration of love and sex—from the pulpit. I did it, and church membership grew by 50 percent. Next, I taught it to a Dallas singles study, and we doubled again.

Then in 2005, as we moved into our new sanctuary, I wanted to teach the book once more. True to form, we drew great crowds. My favorite message in the series comes from chapter 7, on keeping a couple's romance alive. On the Sunday when I was to preach that message, I was suddenly blindsided and engulfed by the most awful and sinister occurrence of my life—that of clinical anxiety and depression.

I had heard about depression and seen others who had been through it, but I had no firsthand knowledge of the affliction. Nor did

I have any knowledge from those close to me. Christians usually do not talk about depression, because believers are—so I thought—not supposed to experience it. Depression is usually seen as a moral failing. To admit to it is to admit weakness and sin.

Upon reflection, I can see I'd had signs of its approach for two years. There were mysterious instances of what I can only describe as a strange and frightening feeling. The problem is that the sensation was unlike anything I had ever felt, so I had no way of knowing what it was. Now I know that it was the approach of anxiety produced by high stress and overwork—an anxiety that would ultimately crescendo into panic attacks and full-blown depression.

I began to notice that in the spring and fall my body would ache. I thought I was developing allergies, but the fact is that while the Christmas season and summertime gave me a chance to rest, church programs always cranked back up in the spring and fall, so the aching would begin again. This was a response to increased adrenaline and stress, but like so many people, I had no clue.

In late May 2006, at 5:30 PM—thirty minutes before the evening service—I was sitting in a chair just as I always did, conversing with people and waiting for the service to begin. From nowhere, in an instant, all my strength went out of me. My body went limp in the chair, my heart rate skyrocketed, and my blood pressure rose so high that I could feel my entire body shake.

I wasn't sure what was happening, so I went to my office and lay down on a couch. In about fifteen minutes, everything subsided, and I went out and preached. I noticed that afterward I had an unquenchably dry mouth. My doctors thought I had become overheated that day when I'd gone for a run and worked in my garden.

Days later, on the evening of my wife's birthday, Teresa and I went out to eat. On the way to a restaurant, we stopped to pay a pastoral visit to an elderly woman in our church. While talking to her, I sensed a strange light-headedness and thought for a moment that I was going to pass out. Next we drove to a Chinese restaurant, and there I felt what I now know was the onset of an anxiety attack or panic attack.

Even if someone told you during a panic attack that you were having one, it would still be terrifying. But when you have no earthly idea of what is happening to you, it is especially dreadful. Anxiety feeds on itself like the perfect storm.

When any part of your body is sick or in pain, your mind is able to stand outside of the pain and appraise it. But when your *mind* is the problem, your very means of perception is amiss. Nothing could be more unsettling. Once my wife and I arrived back home, my legs began to ache so badly that I had to take a hydrocodone to ease the pain and get to sleep.

If you've ever had a stomach virus, you know the awful feeling of nausea building and building until you throw up. The relief is short-lived, because the nausea surges again and again until it runs its course or until medication interrupts the cycle. That was my experience here. Days later I was meeting with David Delk, a fine writer who has worked with me on two of my books. David had flown to Denton to brainstorm with me on some material. It was an important meeting, but I felt worse and worse until I said to him, "I have got to get to a doctor!"

What I was experiencing was a meltdown of anxiety and depression after two years of mounting stress. But at the time, I could not identify what I was feeling, because I had never experienced anything like it. I thought it was the worst flu I had ever caught.

Depression is usually seen as a moral failing.

When I had blood work, urinalysis, and other tests done, I appeared to be perfectly healthy except for a raised blood pressure and heart rate. The leg pains made my doctor suspect diabetes, but tests came back negative. Still I was so frightened that I said to my doctor, "Is there any way I can check into a hospital to get some rest?" The last time I had been in a hospital was for a knee operation in 1972. Since then I had never been more than a hospital visitor, but here I was saying almost involuntarily, "Put me in!"

I might add that by this time I was experiencing one of the worst symptoms of anxiety—the inability to sleep without medication. It had never occurred to me to thank God for a good night's sleep, since I'd always slept well. Now I know it's a blessing given to us at night just as food is by day. But when you cannot get sleep, you start to drown. Anxiety takes away the ability to sleep, which creates more anxiety that further inhibits sleep, and on it goes in a vicious cycle. But again, what compounds it is not knowing what is happening.

It felt as though my accelerator was stuck and my emergency brake was on.

In the hospital, I was given something to stop the growing discomfort in my body and to make me sleep. I don't know what I was thinking—maybe that if I could have a good night of sleep and some relief from the pain, I would be okay the next day.

I *did* feel better. I was able to finish the series on the Song of Solomon at the church, and then I looked ahead to a three-day conference on Romans. Things seemed to relax a bit. But by the next week, like white-capped waves in a growing storm, whatever was threatening to drown me would pull me under.

Steve

Like Tommy, I want to tell you a little bit about myself and explain why I'm qualified to talk about emotional distress. You might assume it's because I have a ministry, called Hope for Life, to those who are hurting emotionally. In the afternoons you can hear me on a radio program out of San Antonio, Texas. Or you might suppose it's because I have a thriving biblical counseling practice for marriage and family issues, and I'm a seminary-trained, ordained minister. I speak to thirty to forty groups a year and produce a great number of teaching CDs. For thirteen years I was privileged to learn from one of the best pastors and teachers in the nation, my co-author Tommy Nelson.

But these credentials are not the real reason I can talk about emotional issues. Rather, it's because I have been there myself.

I have been so anxious that I thought I was going to have to call an ambulance. I have felt as though I were dying. I've been so full of fear, worry, and stress that my body would literally shut down. I know what it's like not to be able to sleep at night because the anxious thoughts running through my mind would not let me rest. I know what it's like to feel so hopeless that the world around me seemed doomed to destruction.

I also know what it is to overcome that stress, to defeat the worry, and to be filled with a sure hope. It is not easy, but it is worth every struggle to find that hope and peace.

Let me back up to the beginning. I grew up on a farm in West Texas near Amarillo, graduated from high school, and went off to the University of North Texas in Denton. There I met the girl of my dreams, Miss Martha Anne Fussell. We fell in love and got married in 1991. By the way, I promised her I was not going to kiss her until I asked her to marry me, and I didn't. I asked her to marry me, kissed her for the first time, and put an engagement ring on her finger. What a time of joy!

We loved being married. We wanted to start a family and were blessed when our son was born in 1995. By the next year, Martha was training for the White Rock Marathon—a lifelong dream of hers. She was an avid athlete and in great condition. In the middle of training, we found out that Martha was pregnant with our second child, and we celebrated again. Martha was given the green light to run the marathon and finished strong. But we didn't know that our lives were about to be turned upside down.

During Martha's training, she had complained to me of chest pain, a pain that made her feel as though something was pushing out on her breastbone. "I guess I need to go see the doctor about it," she said. So we made the appointment, and she went in. It was a short visit; the diagnosis was a strained cartilage. But Martha sensed that something more was wrong.

On a cold, dark January morning, I got a call from the doctor where Martha had just gone for another appointment. "Steve, I need you to come down here so I can talk to you and Martha together." His words filled me with the deepest, darkest fear. I was torn between racing across town to see him and not wanting to go at all for fear of what I might hear.

I entered the examination room with trepidation. My dear Martha sat there as confused and afraid as I was about what the doctor wanted to share. He opened the door and came into the room. It's odd how, in a glance, I read every wrinkle and contortion of his face before he ever said a word.

"Martha, you have a tumor in your chest the size of a small melon. It lies under your sternum, and it is probably fatal. You should see an oncologist immediately."

My beautiful wife was four months pregnant with our second child—a new life growing inside of her—and was dying of cancer.

My first thought was, *What in the world could God be thinking?* We were a young Christian family. We were leading Bible studies, serving in ministry, and I was attending seminary. We had a one-and-a-half-year-old son and another precious child on the way. *We have great plans to serve the Lord. This just does not make sense. God, You must have made a mistake.*

Martha, reading me like a book, took my hand and said words I will never forget: "Steve, I know we don't understand, but God is bigger than this. He is in control, and His control is perfect. No matter what happens, it is His will, and His will is the safest place to be."

Anything that feels like the end of the world is not what it appears to be.

My heart melted at the strength of this mighty woman of God. Martha had just heard the same words from the doctor that I had heard, yet her response was so different. I was overwhelmed by her courage. We both broke down and wept openly. We immediately prayed for God to heal her and for Him to be glorified in whatever He was going to do. I had never prayed so soberly in my life.

God is perfect. Nothing happens outside the will of God, and to be in God's will is the safest place to be. Those truths were the theme of our life together. No matter what circumstance God had placed us in, we could find peace and joy in knowing that He was sovereign. I am not talking about happiness; that's different. I am talking about pure joy in the Lord.

Martha and I were both asked many times how we remained so peaceful and kept from being angry at God. Our answer was always the same: When you know who you are in light of who God is, and you know who God is and begin to understand His sovereignty, then you can find peace and joy.

But trusting God did not mean we were unaffected emotionally. Martha was one of the healthiest people I knew, and this news blindsided us. While I had always wrestled with anxiety, it had been fairly manageable up to that point. The level of anxiety that hit me next knocked me off my feet.

Meanwhile, we had a big decision to make. What do you do when you have cancer and are pregnant at the same time? The doctors told us we should abort the fetus right away, because they were convinced that our baby could not survive the chemotherapy. Then get on with the treatment, they said.

But this was not just a fetus to us! It was our child whom God knew, even though he or she had not yet been born. Our child's days were already numbered by God, and we weren't about to let a doctor change that. After much prayer, we decided to begin the chemo and trust that God would protect our child.

Martha endured eight rounds of the harshest chemotherapy you can go through. Imagine the stress of being pregnant, receiving chemotherapy, and having a toddler to care for all at once. It was a hard, stressful time, but we managed to make some good memories.

In June 1997 our precious little daughter, Madison, was born at three pounds and fourteen ounces. We were able to take her home from the hospital in three days, and she was completely normal and healthy. After eight rounds of chemo, that was nothing short of a miracle. God had brought our daughter safely through.

Even while we celebrated the arrival of Madison, we were faced with the hard truth that Martha was not going to recover. A sonogram showed that the chemotherapy had not stopped the cancer from spreading into all of Martha's abdomen.

When someone we love has cancer, the fear of loss is strong. That fear had never really left me from the day Martha received her diagnosis, but now her death was becoming reality. I remember selfishly praying over and over, "God, please don't take her home; leave her here for me and the kids. I don't want to be alone."

Martha died just a few months later. The Lord took her home, and I was left to be a mommy and a daddy to a two-year-old and a four-month-old. It's difficult to describe how hard it all was—grief and anxiety and a broken heart, all with the demands of a newborn and toddler. I was a mess.

Of course, I was still seeking God and feeling His presence. I read my Bible every day and prayed. I had friends and good counsel around me. I even had my thinking pretty straight. My head seemed clear.

But my body took all the stress, grief, and anxiety and just decided to shut down. My heart would race, and my chest hurt. I couldn't breathe; it felt as though I were drowning. My whole body would shake, and I had terrible headaches. My stomach and esophagus would burn and give me diarrhea.

Always I felt an extreme sense of doom and despair, as though everything was wrong and destruction loomed like a dark cloud. I actually thought I was dying, and the fear of leaving my two children made me feel even worse. I stayed in this wretched state for another eighteen months, living with fear and dread every day.

This is why I can talk about emotional distress now. Whether you're having heart palpitations, constricted breathing, obsessive thoughts of dying, or absolute, uncontrolled anxiety, I've been there. I get it! I can walk you through this because I have been in the dark valley of anxiety and despair and have made it to the other side, where healing and peace are found.

This is the wonderful news I have for you: You're not crazy, and you're not dying. I know it can feel like that. Your mind can run to terrifyingly dark places, and your body can convince you that you're not going to make it. But you will. Just hang on with Tommy and me through this book, and you will learn how to get through it. You can survive and even recover.

Remember this: Anything that feels like the end of the world is not what it appears to be. Have hope. God is the God of hope. He is not a God of fear, worry, and stress. Grab onto His hope like a lifeline, and cling to it.

TWO

Deeper & Deeper

Anxiety, obsessions, fear . . . and Scripture

Tommy

I'd been through some scary weeks, but like an athlete, I simply patched it, took a pill, got a shot, gave it a rest, and then went back at it full bore. People were waiting and expecting. The pressure was on, and I had to come through.

It was the way I liked it. Anyone doing something that matters performs under expectations, standards, and pressure. But what happened the next week was worse. It was beyond my power to will, to endure, or to fix. It was the most frightening, dark, hopeless pit I could imagine falling into.

My wife and I and our two grandchildren had come back home after a trip to the zoo. We were sitting in the living room when all of a sudden the bottom dropped out beneath me. Not physically, as it had a couple of weeks earlier, but in a different way. The closest I can come to explaining it is that something collapsed "metaphysically"—in my mind or soul or spirit or emotions or endocrine system or chemical makeup or brain activity or whatever. Here was an enemy I didn't even know existed, much less could overcome.

I began to feel myself sinking into the ocean depths, into a black hole or emotionless wasteland where I was disconnected from everything around me. It seemed as though I was sliding into a netherworld, an in-between dimension. All I was aware of was growing fear. The anxiety I had tasted earlier was now back in a more intense and sinister way. The question occurred to me, *Am I losing my mind?* I had never considered such a thing before.

Control is a large part of our lives. We all grasp for privacy, health, and independence—all factors of control. To men, I think it is even *more* important. For some reason, I have always been the quarterback, the captain, the pastor. I've always taken charge. I like to walk alone, and that is why what was happening now seemed so frustrating.

This wasn't a pain I could deaden myself. I had no control. I had no say in what was occurring. It was not even a pain or illness in my body as I understood *body* to mean. This was a problem in my mind, emotions, and very means of perception. I could go on with a leg missing or even a prognosis of certain death. But this? It was absolutely debilitating. My life as I knew it was out of my hands.

The emotionless void and growing anxiety continued to engulf me. All who were close to me admonished me to get checked out thoroughly to make sure that everything had been done to locate the problem. So I lined up a full physical at the Cooper Clinic in Dallas.

By this time, sleep on my own was impossible. Ambien could knock me out, but at about 3 AM, I could feel the physical and emotional anxiety crawl onto me like a dark cloud or a sinister presence. I still had no paradigm to be able to say, "This is stress-based anxiety and depression." I had no frame of reference, which is what made it more frightening.

Here was an enemy I didn't even know existed.

My tests at the clinic showed me to be in perfect health except for my blood pressure. But the woman who did the examination said, "You are obviously in a state of anxiety. For the short term, you might try Xanax." At these words, everything in me revolted. My first thought was, *Xanax is what the college girls in my church take when they can't cope with life.* As wrong as that now sounds, it is what went through my mind. There was no way I was going to stoop to taking a sedative.

Doing nothing was not a option either, because I knew something was terribly wrong with me. I had honestly been hoping that in the five hours of examination they would find a problem. I'd have given anything to know it was a tumor or blockage or stroke or hormonal imbalance or something else I could blame for sucking me into this hole. Because of this, my heart almost leaped for joy when the doctor added as an aside, "Now we *did* find your thyroxine to be somewhat low." *Aha!* I thought. *A hormone! I knew it!*

I said to the doctor some words that I could not believe were coming out of me: "I can't go back home!" It was simply a cry for help. Everybody was saying I was healthy, but I knew something horrible was happening to me, and someone needed to recognize it.

Once again, I checked into a hospital. More tests were done. An endocrinologist analyzed my thyroid. It's funny, but each time I checked into a hospital, I had an immediate sense of relief just knowing that I would get help and that people were looking for whatever was causing the mysterious sense of anxiety. The hospital gave me Ativan, a standard anti-anxiety medication that might help me sleep and give me a little relief from the horrid, ever-growing anxiety that was rapidly dragging me down. The result was that I had a short-term sense of relief and a return to being "me." They continued to run tests, and an MRI revealed an infection in one of my sinuses. Although the thyroid concern turned up negative, in place of it was a hope that the infection had been causing my symptoms.

Three days later, I checked out, thinking the heavy antibiotics they gave me for the infection might help me come up for air and get back to normal. My hopes would be dashed a couple of days later.

Steve

I've shared what I went through in dealing with the illness and death of my wife, but anxiety and stress do not always have such dire triggers. Daily life provides plenty of opportunities.

I've spent the last couple of weeks working hard on this book, particularly in the last few days. Yesterday, I returned from fishing with my boys in the morning to find that my oldest daughter had been using my laptop and had run down the battery. No problem, except my laptop reset to three days ago, losing all my most recent work. I was devastated.

Why? Because attention deficit disorder and I go hand in hand, and I usually have only one bullet in the creative chamber. I also desire my world to be very ordered, keeping things right where I want them. I don't do well with unforeseen change and matters that are out of my control. Losing my work reshuffled my deck, and I was none too happy. I spent an hour of so in distress and frustration. I grumped at my family and felt overwhelmed.

This was the way I used to live all the time—needing my world to be just as I wished. Now, though, I'm able to move through my frustration more quickly and get to a better place. Not perfect, but so much better. Life is not always going to play by our rules. The key to managing ourselves in the midst of everyday frustrations is to look to Scripture. There we can find what we need to experience peace, joy, rest, contentment, and hope.

Believe it or not, the Bible has a lot to say about emotional distress, especially in the areas of anxiety, obsessive-compulsive behavior, and depression. You have probably tried to get better in your own way. You might have even spent money on doctors and psychiatrists and counselors, and you're still not better. If you're reading this, there is hope. Let's look at what God has to say about these three areas.

First, on anxiety, Scripture is clear.

Be anxious for nothing, but in everything by prayer and supplication with thanksgiving, let your requests be made known to God, and the peace of God, which surpasses all comprehension, will guard your hearts and your minds in Christ Jesus. (Philippians 4:6–7, NASB)

Humble yourselves, therefore, under God's mighty hand, that he may lift you up in due time. Cast all your anxiety on him because he cares for you. (1 Peter 5:6–7, NIV)

"Therefore I say to you, do not worry about your life, what you will eat or what you will drink; nor about your body, what you will put on. Is not life more than food and the body more than clothing?" (Matthew 6:25)

For God has not given us a spirit of fear, but of power and of love and of a sound mind. (2 Timothy 1:7)

Anxiety, worry, fear . . . do these emotions sound familiar to you?

After Martha died, my anxiety ballooned into full-blown hypochondria—worrying about my body, about what ailment I had, or what could be fatal inside of me. Yet Scripture tells me that I'm not to worry about my health or my future. In Matthew 6, Jesus went on to say, "Therefore do not worry about tomorrow, for tomorrow will worry about its own things. Sufficient for the day is its own trouble." (verse 34).

Looking back at my laptop incident, I was able to stop and reason with myself. The truth was that if I lost all my work, life would go on. My world was not over. I also realized that I might be able to recover the files. Those were truths, and they set me free.

The lie I initially believed was that this mishap could be nearly life-threatening, and I could not have peace when such things happened. I believed the lie that I could not recreate what I had written, and on and on. My brain went into a panic, which released adrenaline, which gave me the false impression that everything was doomed.

The Bible has a lot to say about emotional distress.

But this was a lie. I was able to walk myself through the Scriptures quoted earlier and bring myself back to a healthy place, which my family was glad about.

Second, what about obsessive-compulsive behavior? When we obsess, and obsess, and obsess, we eventually wear down our bodies to the point where the body just doesn't work anymore. If you are obsessive, your mind constantly runs away with you to a dark place, dwelling on the extreme and horrific. Instead, we're told:

> Finally, brethren, whatever is true, whatever is honorable, whatever
> is right, whatever is pure, whatever is lovely, whatever is of good
> repute, if there is any excellence, and if anything worthy of praise,
> let your mind dwell on these things. (Philippians 4:8, NASB)

We are to let our minds ponder what is right and pure and lovely. We are commanded to train ourselves to think about these things—about what God wants us to center on, not about what our brains run to that causes such distress. Proverbs 3:5–6 (NIV) says,

> Trust in the LORD with all your heart
>> and lean not on your own understanding;
> in all your ways acknowledge him,
>> and he will make your paths straight.

Understanding implies that we feel a need to be in control or to make sense of something before we can rest. We think that when we are in control, we can keep life in the order *we* want. This is all about self. We are keeping order in our world so that we will be comfortable, often at the expense of others.

The other day a client told me she was ready for divorce. Every day when her husband came home, he would walk in the front door barking instructions on how the house should be. Shoes weren't ordered by the front door. The trim above the bathroom door didn't pass the white-glove test. There was a dirty dish in the sink.

His words were, "Haven't you done anything all day?" He didn't ask how the piano lessons went, how long the pickup line at school was, how the doctor visit turned out, or how she managed to grocery shop and get dinner made in between all those other things. He only cared about what was important to *him!*

That's a classic case of someone who selfishly needs everything in his world to be the way he wants it, or else he is unhappy and makes everyone around him miserable. He may get his world the way he wants it, but he will be alone in it.

We must trust God enough not to have to understand. The way you trust God is to give the situation over to Him. I had to give losing my work over to Him and trust that He would walk me through it. This starts with spending time in God's Word. The more you read your Bible, the more you'll know God. The more you know God, the more you will trust Him. The more you trust Him, the more you will experience peace, joy, rest, hope, and contentment.

Finally, what about depression? Rest assured that depression is talked about in Scripture. God understands and often addresses depression.

In Psalm 42, David is having a my-spirit-battles-my-flesh moment with himself and says, "Why are you in despair, O my soul? And why have you become disturbed within me?" (NASB).

Have you ever felt disturbed? Have you ever been in despair?

After asking himself why he is in despair, David tells his soul, "Hope in God, for I shall again praise Him for the help of His presence. O my God, my soul is in despair within me; therefore I remember You from the land of the Jordan and the peaks of Hermon" (verses 5–6, NASB)

Then in Psalm 22:1, we see David asking the familiar questions, "My God, my God, why have you forsaken me? Why are you so far from saving me, so far from the words of my groaning?" (NIV) He's saying, "God, where are You? I feel as though You've abandoned me."

I can't tell you how many depressed people I've counseled who say, "I feel like God has abandoned me." They think He has just left them alone to suffer. This is a lie. Scripture says that God is always near believers; we don't have to feel alone in our distress.

Clearly, anxiety, obsession, and depression are not new to the twenty-first century. Since the fall of man, we see humans having to struggle with such things. Listen to Cain:

> And Cain said to the LORD, "My punishment is greater than I can
> bear! Surely You have driven me out this day from the face of the
> ground; I shall be hidden from Your face; I shall be a fugitive and
> a vagabond on the earth, and it will happen that anyone who finds
> me will kill me." (Genesis 4:13–14)

Cain's despair was brought on by his own doing, which can happen with us too, but sometimes God allows suffering for His own purposes and our good. Either way, God knows that we suffer and hurt and even despair, so He addresses it. We have to be willing to allow Scripture to help us understand our situation as well as to comfort us in it.

Sometimes that comfort comes in the form of peace in the midst of the storm, and other times it's protection from the storm. In one instance, Christ woke up from His nap on a boat and calmed the storm for His worried disciples. Another time, He walked out on the water to the disciples in a storm and brought the boat safely to shore while leaving the storm alone.

The important point is that peace, rest, joy, contentment, and hope are found in the Bible. Be willing to accept God's help in the way He chooses. You may ask God to solve your problem, but beware of wanting to have it solved only your way. You may want the storm to go away, but God may choose to carry you safely through the storm while letting it rage around you. You have to be willing to trust God in the midst of the storm.

A teenager came to me in a spiritual crisis. Mom and Dad had sent her to me because they felt they were losing her both emotionally and spiritually, and they were right.

She was mature and a deep thinker (which hadn't always served her well). She looked deep into my eyes, hoping I could give her some answers to her questions. "If God loves me, then why have I had such terrible things happen to me?" "If God is real, why won't He answer my prayers?" "Am I just a toy for God to play and experiment with? Is He messing with me for His own enjoyment?"

In her self-centeredness, this young lady was demanding that God do what she wanted in order for her to play the game. God had not chosen to take away her storm, so she assumed He was not answering her prayers.

The truth is, God simply didn't answer her prayers the way she wanted Him to. Her healing came when she realized that God might allow her to suffer and wanted her to trust Him in the midst of the storm. I could see the lights come on as she began to understand her life from God's perspective, rather than from her selfish teenage perspective.

So many Christians are struggling or have struggled with emotional distress. God knows where you are, and He won't leave you there. He has given His words. Be patient. Be faithful. Be courageous. Be at peace!

THREE

Sunk!

Trials, tribulations, suffering . . . and Scripture

Tommy

After three days in the hospital, I felt some rest and relief from the growing depression. I had taken a break from preaching on Sundays, but on the horizon was the 800-person conference on the book of Romans.

The conference was going to be taped for a high-quality video series. The people coming had paid for admission. We had breakfast burritos, chilled Dr Pepper, and great coffee and kolaches. It was a special kind of a conference called "Romans, Texas Style."

The pressure was on. In twelve sessions, I would teach a book that I normally take a year of Sundays to preach. I had done a meticulous verse-by-verse notation above the biblical text for all the people to follow. It would be a chance—after thirty years of study—to take perhaps the most important book of the Bible and get it down for people to watch on screen. That is why it was even *more* distressing that the creeping black cloud of depression chose this very moment to move back in.

The most important attribute in all the world to me is *duty*—fulfilling one's responsibility. So this was like getting the flu fifteen minutes before game time. It was something I couldn't control. I could preach in a cast or from a gurney, but not when in the grip of this "thing" that was struggling for control of my life.

It was a Sunday, just five days before people would arrive from all over the country. My hope was that as "game time" approached, my body would rise to the challenge, adrenaline would kick in, and I would muscle my way through Romans. Then maybe I could take some serious time off in the summer. But that Sunday night something went terribly wrong.

That night, sleep was impossible. At about 2 AM, an intense heightening of anxiety (although I still had not defined it as such) jolted me awake. All I knew was that it was a god-awful feeling I could only call sinister. It was as though something was hijacking my being. I read a book until about 6 AM, then I tried to go to sleep again. But another jolt of distress hit me, rousing me from bed.

I went outside to take a walk up and down the sidewalk. The feeling was building in intensity, like whitewater rapids or a raging sea. As I walked, I recited Scripture—Psalm 23, Romans 8—constantly looking to God as this whatever-it-was enveloped me.

My wife, Teresa, was up by now and said we should go out for breakfast to take my mind off of what was happening to me. As she dressed in the bedroom and I walked in the den, the anxiety hit like a full-blown tornado.

I had heard of the term *panic attack*, but it was always something that could happen to someone else, not me. Your body reacts to continual stress by going into a fight-or-flight response. All your blood goes into the legs, and your vision becomes tunneled. You become light-headed, and your blood pressure skyrockets. The anxiety crests to first-class panic for no reason whatsoever.

> *Your first thought is that you are losing your mind.*

Your first thought is that you are losing your mind. The attack lasts only for twenty minutes or so and then begins to subside, but it leaves an aftereffect called *anxiety disorder*, because you are constantly worried about the attack recurring. The worst part is that if a panic attack is a 10, then the continuing anxiety is a 6. It's like a persistent toothache.

And the anxiety is only half of it. The other side of the coin is clinical depression. It is a black hole where all emotion seems to be removed from you. The worst part, though, is that you have nothing to compare it to. You simply have no clue what is wrong. This all started with me at eight o'clock on that Monday morning in June 2006.

By nine that morning, I was sitting on my patio with my heart crying out to God. In four days, 800 people would show up for Romans, and here I was, not able even to sit still for thirty seconds. I was in a constant state of agitation, with no ability to sleep or even think straight. Two months earlier, my paths, as Job put it, "were bathed in butter," and now I was like Jonah, "beneath the roots of the mountains" in the belly of the beast.

"Why, O God?" was all my heart could cry out. "What have I done?" Why on the eve of one of the greatest contributions I could make to the cause of Christ—the exposition of Romans on video—would I be knocked down like this? A tempest had swept in over the waters, and I couldn't swim any longer.

Steve

Whenever we are struggling, we have a natural tendency to question God. "Why God? Where are You, God?" or "What are You thinking, God?" David once said:

> My God, My God, why have You forsaken Me?
> Why are You so far from helping Me,
> And from the words of My groaning?
> O My God, I cry in the daytime, but You do not hear;
> And in the night season, and am not silent. (Psalm 22:1–2)

The Bible says that David was a man after God's own heart. He was a deeply faithful man whom God loved, and yet he still felt this way about his times of suffering. It seems we are not so different.

I had never really understood the concept of suffering until my wife passed away in an untimely manner. No one close to me had ever died. I had never had any health issues. I was blessed with a great childhood and an awesome family. I had never really been chiseled on by God. When I say I had never had to deal with true suffering, I mean it. Life had been easy.

That all changed with my wife's cancer diagnosis. Nothing had prepared me for that, and I had to adapt quickly or sink. I sank. Eight months into the fight with Martha's cancer, I got a visit from my pastor, Tommy Nelson, at one of the darkest moments of my life. Martha was in surgery and wasn't expected to make it through. Tommy put his arm around me in the ICU waiting room and told me something that changed my life. I expected him to give me a typical pastor's speech, but all he said was, "She's God's. He loves her more than you do; trust Him." Then he walked away.

At that moment, despite all my seminary training, all my biblical knowledge, and all my spiritual maturity, I became an infant just learning to walk. What Tommy told me changed my earthly thinking—my earthly fears—into a heavenly way of thinking about things. When I looked at my situation from God's perspective, things appeared so different.

We see things dimly here on earth, but God has a vast view of us and our life. A thousand days are like one to Him. We think we get shorted if we die thirty or forty years prematurely, but thirty or forty years are like a blink of an eye to Him. He knows what we don't, so we must learn to trust Him with what we don't understand.

> Trust in the LORD with all your heart,
> and lean not on your own understanding. (Proverbs 3:5)

Aha! I get it now.

Martha died four months later, but those four months were much more peaceful for me than when Martha first got sick. I was able to say, "I love her, Lord, and I don't want her to go, but she is Yours. You can have her if You want. I won't fight You on it. Thy will and not my own."

I had never understood suffering until my wife passed away.

It is important for us to adopt a biblical perspective on trials, tribulations, and suffering. What trial are you fighting God on? Is there a tribulation that threatens to separate you from the comforting arm of your heavenly Father? What suffering are you unwilling to submit to?

Shadrach, Meshach, and Abednego were thrown into a fiery furnace by the king of Babylon (see Daniel 3). The Bible text tells us that when they went into the furnace, they were bound by ropes. When they came out of the furnace, not a hair or anything on their bodies was burned except the ropes that had bound them. Sometimes we have to go through the fire for God to burn away the things that bind us.

We may find ourselves in the midst of a trial for a number of reasons:

1. *We have brought it on ourselves.* This happens when we have behaved in a foolish or sinful way. The discipline of God or the consequences of our actions cause us difficulties.

No discipline seems pleasant at the time, but painful. Later on, however, it produces a harvest of righteousness and peace for those who have been trained by it. (Hebrews 12:11, NIV)

2. *Circumstances beyond our control are causing our suffering.* This could be anything from a medical condition that causes depression, anxiety, or some other sort of emotional distress, to the loss of a loved one, rejection, abandonment, or mistreatment by others.

3. *God is allowing a trial to mold and shape us.* Sometimes God lets tribulation happen to us not because of sin or anything we have done, but because of what He has done or is doing. This is evident in the passage below.

As he [Jesus] went along, he saw a man blind from birth. His disciples asked him, "Rabbi, who sinned, this man or his parents, that he was born blind?"

"Neither this man nor his parents sinned," said Jesus, "but this happened so that the work of God might be displayed in his life." (John 9:1–3, NIV)

No matter what the cause, we must keep a healthy, truthful perspective on trials, tribulations, and suffering. Look at what else Scripture says:

In this you greatly rejoice, though now for a little while you may have had to suffer grief in all kinds of trials. These have come so that your faith—of greater worth than gold, which perishes even though refined by fire—may be proved genuine and may result in praise, glory and honor when Jesus Christ is revealed. (1 Peter 1:6–7, NIV)

Consider it pure joy, my brothers, whenever you face trials of many kinds, because you know that the testing of your faith develops perseverance. Perseverance must finish its work so that you may be mature and complete, not lacking anything. (James 1:2–4, NIV)

And we know that in all things God works for the good of those who love him, who have been called according to his purpose. (Romans 8:28, NIV)

Beloved, do not think it strange concerning the fiery trial which is to try you, as though some strange thing happened to you; but rejoice to the extent that you partake of Christ's sufferings, that when His glory is revealed, you may also be glad with exceeding joy. (1 Peter 4:12–13)

We also glory in tribulations, knowing that tribulation produces perseverance; and perseverance, character; and character, hope. Now hope does not disappoint, because the love of God has been poured out in our hearts by the Holy Spirit who was given to us. (Romans 5:3–5)

Notice, by the way, that nowhere in the previous passages is Satan mentioned. Many Christians automatically say that they are being attacked by Satan when things are difficult. Yes, Scripture does say that Satan seeks to destroy us, but most Bible passages on trials do not mention this at all. They speak of God allowing trials for His own purposes. Let's not give Satan more airtime than we should.

We also know that God desires to use our trials for His glory and for others. We should be willing to see how our suffering prepares us to minister to others who suffer.

> Blessed be the God and Father of our Lord Jesus Christ, the Father
> of mercies and God of all comfort, who comforts us in all our
> tribulation, that we may be able to comfort those who are in any
> trouble, with the comfort with which we ourselves are comforted
> by God. (2 Corinthians 1:3–4)

One more lesson from Scripture is important. Often in the middle of our distress, we feel as though we just can't go on. In my counseling office, it's common for me to hear things like "I can't take it anymore" or "This is more than I can bear." The truth is that God will not give you more than you can bear.

> No temptation has seized you except what is common to man. And
> God is faithful; he will not let you be tempted beyond what you
> can bear. But when you are tempted, he will also provide a way out
> so that you can stand up under it. (1 Corinthians 10:13, NIV)

A gentleman whom I counsel had been struggling for three months with deep depression. He was successful for many years, but the weight of work, other responsibilities, and guilt finally took over. He literally woke up one day and could not get out of bed because of depression. At 53, he was very broken, but he gave his life to the Lord and started the process of healing. I worked intently with him on his thinking, forgiveness, God's grace, and the hope that the Lord offered him. He got on antidepressants and started understanding who he was in light of who God is.

When I saw him yesterday, I gave him a hug and asked how he was. He looked me in the eye and said, "Fantastic!" All I had heard from him for three months was, "I feel terrible," "I can't go on like this," "I am so depressed," and so on. To hear "Fantastic!" was amazing. He said he felt alive again, and he had hope.

If it weren't for the suffering he went through, he may never have come to know the Lord. God used a trial to bring this man to salvation.

What is God doing in your life now? Don't waste a good trial.

PART TWO

questions from the depths of despair

FOUR

How Did I Get Here?

Identifying the source of your depression

Tommy

My wife said I reminded her of the horse Barbaro, who won the 2006 Kentucky Derby but then broke his leg at the start of the Preakness Stakes two weeks later. The race was over for him, but he just kept trying to run. Finally, they had to tie his foreleg to his upper leg so he would not hurt himself further. As painful and fruitless as his attempt was, I know why he did it. He was trained to run. He was expected to run.

So was I. A church of 4,000 with a five-million-dollar budget and eight million dollars remaining on a building loan beckoned, along with conferences and engagements and books and videos and preaching and study guides and Young Guns and other marvelous responsibilities or possibilities. I was trained to run and expected to run. I also love to run. My favorite expression by a coach is said to have come from Vince Lombardi: "Life is lying exhausted in victory on the field of competition." I had always wanted something for which I could be totally expended, and Christ and His cause were worth it. I just did not realize how close I would come to "lying exhausted."

The Monday that a panic attack engulfed me left me with an acute sense of anxiety; I couldn't sit, nap, rest, or read. I could not communicate with other people. I could not watch a TV show. My legs felt as though electricity was running through them. My wife would rub them and feel the muscle fibers crackling and firing.

I read an account of another man who went through anxiety, and he said that the Fourth of July was going off under his skin. It was like a body hung in fifth gear. My body had reacted to emotional overwork and said, "That's all." The thought crossed my mind with horror, *Is this a nervous breakdown?* I, for sure, was nervous. And I most assuredly had broken down.

Out of sheer desperation, I called my doctor just so I could have some sense of control and not feel caught in the vortex of this cyclone. Once again, all signs showed me to be in perfect health, save for high blood pressure. I went back home, and I discovered something odd about a panic attack—you fall asleep afterward out of sheer emotional exhaustion.

When I awoke, my friend Doug Hudson was there. Doug had organized all the Song of Solomon Conferences and helped with all my books. I count him one of my closest friends. He also was organizing our "Romans, Texas Style," where we would videotape the verse-by-verse exposition of Romans. It was just "Black Monday." I could not see myself speaking even with one person in private, let alone 800 people in public. But Friday was coming, and the conference would start.

Doug said to me, "Look, let's just cancel the conference now and take our losses." This sounded great to me, but that night I took a sleeping pill, got a good night's sleep, and woke up feeling better. So I called Doug and said, "Let's do it after all!" Just as my wife said, I was like Barbaro at the races, doing anything I could to continue. But by that night, the anxiety and depression had come back.

I called the elders of my church together and confessed to them that I was toast and could not keep going. I told them I needed at least three months off to rest and try to get rid of whatever it was that had me in its grip. These men were with me all the way. They took all the pressure off of me and said that anything I needed would be provided. I truly don't know what I would've done without them.

It was as if the anxiety had drained all the life out of me.

Not only did I call off the Romans conference, but I was going to have to call off the upcoming Song of Solomon conferences too, and that was hard for me. It wasn't just the loss of income, which was real, but it was also the failure on my part to follow through on a duty. Once I dropped the conferences, however, it felt as though a tremendous load had been lifted off of me.

I began to find out some things about anxiety and depression—far more than I ever thought I needed to know. *The culprit is stress.* Stress makes the body run on adrenaline, which is okay for a short time but not over a long period, because adrenaline produces cortisol, and cortisol inhibits the proper production and use of serotonin—a neurotransmitter that makes your brain function as it should. What has to be done is to locate the source of stress and begin to eliminate it.

In my case, it was easy to identify the problem—overwork—and then eliminate it by tossing everything off my schedule. But even when you've removed the source, the horrific symptoms of depression and anxiety continue. They must ebb away like flood waters—slowly and steadily—and that can be distressing .

For all of June and July, that process consumed me. I discovered that it is important to talk to someone who has gone through depression or a professional who has experience in treating depression. Someone needs to explain medically what is happening. Someone needs to tell you that he or she has been through it and that *you* will make it also.

It is terrifying when your mind—your very means of perception—becomes impaired. We sometimes think of the mind as some objective, free mechanism that floats outside of sensory data and informs us about the world we are in. The fact is, our mind operates within an organ—the brain—and is fallen like every part of our being. It can become impaired, and that is scary.

For two months, I was always exhausted. I went from running four miles a day and lifting weights at a gym every day to not being able to lift at all and finding the energy to walk on a treadmill for only thirty minutes at a time. It was as if the anxiety had drained all the life out of me.

During the day, I could rarely sit for over a minute or so, because my legs felt as though they were just awakening after "falling asleep." They would crackle with electricity and felt normal only when my wife rubbed them.

Reading was nearly impossible, because my mind simply could not rest upon a page or sentence and think on it. My greatest joy in life was my Bible, yet I could not read it for over thirty seconds. I couldn't read a paper or even watch TV, because my mind would not stay on a subject. But I discovered the depth of God's mercy through other means than reading.

For example, one thing God did was to allow my son John, who played Triple A minor league baseball for the Memphis Redbirds, an affiliate of the St. Louis Cardinals, to begin having a tremendous year of baseball at the very time that my anxiety was reaching a crest. John had a hitting streak in which it seemed the ball was flying out of the park with regularity. My wife and I watched him on a computer feed, and whenever he made a great play or got a hit, we would rejoice.

For some reason, nighttime's approach gave me comfort, because I knew a sleeping pill would give me some brief relief. My body would relax before sleep, and I could lie there and finally read. What I read was Charles Spurgeon's devotional *Morning and Evening*. This famous preacher had been through depression, and somehow I felt comfort from him a century removed.

I would fall asleep at about ten, and then at three in the morning, I could literally feel the anxiety crawl onto me. Natural sleep was now impossible, as were naps. For four months, I did not fall asleep without help from medication.

I would go by my church at times and see the beautiful complex that I had struggled and sacrificed for during the past thirty years, and now I could not even enter in among its people. My work, labor, sacrifice, and dreams had been swept away in this storm.

Instead I dreamed about receiving a phone call from the hospital saying that I had an absence of some hormone or *something* that would explain what was happening. That call never came. I just sat and hurt within.

My wife was my safe person. People going through depression usually have a safe person or safe place where the depression feels lighter. Sometimes Teresa would go to shop for groceries, and I would follow along with her like a handicapped child—which is what I was. I had withdrawn into my own despair.

But God continued to touch me in ways that went beyond the Scriptures I could not read.

One day, I was puttering in my garden—something I could do to relieve the stress. I was singing to myself the words of an old gospel hymn that Ethel Waters and others had recorded: "His eye is on the sparrow, and I know He watches me." Just as I was singing it, I looked at my feet and found a dead sparrow in among the flowers. The only thing I could think of were our Savior's words about how God knows every sparrow that falls. It was as though the Lord was saying, "I know where you are. I know how you hurt. I am right here with you."

A second incident also happened while I was gardening. Teresa asked me to get a wheelbarrow, and when I did, I saw that a cicada was clinging to the back of one handle. A cicada is a locust-like insect that sheds its outer skin like a snake. It leaves the hard shell on a tree or, in this case, a wheelbarrow. I had seen many cicada shells, but never the cicada that emerged from it. It was spectacular—purple, vermillion, teal, and every other color you can imagine. I looked at the old and the new side by side, and then the cicada flew away. Again it seemed as though God was saying, "I know the plans I have for you . . . plans to give you hope and a future" (Jeremiah 29:11, NIV).

A short while later, I heard my Jack Russell terrier named Buddy barking and jumping around my screen-enclosed back porch, because he had trapped something. It was a hummingbird that had flown in through the open screen door and could not find its way out. Time and time again it flew into one invisible barrier and then another. Below him, Buddy was expecting the bird to exhaust itself and fall into his waiting jaws. I tried to help the little bird, but it flew away from me. Finally, when it was completely spent, I took it in my hands. A hummingbird is amazingly small and delicate when you look at one up close. It lay still in my hands. I took it outside, and once it revived in the light, I let it go.

I felt much the same before God. I was trapped in a place I could not see, understand, or escape from. All around me was despair and death, and the only One who could help me was the One I now feared most, wondering if I had offended Him in some way. And yet, I sensed that somehow, someday, I too would be released to new life.

Sparrows, bugs, and hummingbirds can sometimes be as comforting as all the truth written.

Steve

A number of people in the Bible struggled with emotional distress, including Job, Elijah (1 Kings 19), King Saul (1 Samuel 16:14–23), Jeremiah, and, of course, David. He was very open with God about his emotional distress. Once he said, "I am troubled, I am bowed down greatly; I go mourning all the day long. . . . I groan because of the turmoil of my heart" (Psalm 38:6, 8).

I got to wondering how many of the psalms in the Bible talk about pain, depression, and hopelessness. Look at this list!

Psalm 6, 13, 18, 23, 25, 27, 31, 32, 34, 37, 38, 39, 40, 42, 43, 46, 51, 55, 62, 63, 69, 71, 73, 77, 84, 86, 90, 91, 94, 95, 103, 104, 107, 110, 116, 118, 121, 123, 124, 130, 138, 139, 141, 142, 143, 146, 147

Most people in Scripture were emotionally distressed because of external oppression or, in some cases, their own sin. But we know that you can also be depressed for other reasons. Sometimes your body is just not producing enough serotonin. It may not be the result of sin or poor choices on your part; it is simply that your body quit doing what it was supposed to do.

Donna had originally come to see me for depression. I later determined that it was really anxiety that felt like depression because of the hopelessness that accompanied it. We spent about four sessions trying to get to the root of her emotional distress. She continued to say that it was because of her controlling, mean husband. He *was* controlling and mean, but I just had the sense it was more than that.

I decided to try something out of the ordinary. I would spend a whole session having her tell me about every detail of her life up to this point. She was resistant and finally blurted out, "Okay, fine, I'll tell some stuff about me, but it doesn't matter. I am over all my past stuff!" She went on to tell me that she had been sexually abused throughout her childhood and forced to become a prostitute at age sixteen. Then she had continued in high-end prostitution for twenty years, often having sex with ten men a day and working almost every day. For twenty years! You do the math. In addition, she had submitted to many abortions.

Sometimes your body is just not producing enough serotonin.

Donna was a mature Christian now, with children, a husband, and a fairly normal life. So she couldn't figure out why she was still under emotional distress. It became clear to me that she had not dealt with her past or accepted God's forgiveness. She was riddled with guilt and shame, and the worst part was that she refused to believe it. Once she saw the truth, she began to get better. It got worse before it got better, but it *did* get better.

You see why it is important to figure out what is causing your depression? I don't think it is necessary to spend weeks and weeks exploring your past, but it *is* helpful to understand why you are struggling.

- If you're feeling guilt, shame, or conviction of sin, then you can resolve it.
- If your environment or circumstances are weighing you down, then you can change your lifestyle and priorities.
- If you are overtaxing your body and mind, then you can reduce your stressors.
- If there seems to be no reason that you or the people around you can discern, then you can still address your condition medically. No matter the cause, your body has probably stopped producing enough of the right chemicals, leaving you depressed.

(By the way, don't confuse depression with grief. I hear people all the time who say "I'm depressed" when actually they are grieving the loss of something. Grief is much different from depression but can symptomatically look the same.)

What does the Bible say about depression that is the result of sin? Early on we have the example of Cain:

> Then the LORD said to Cain, "Why are you angry? Why is your face downcast? If you do what is right, will you not be accepted? But if you do not do what is right, sin is crouching at your door; it desires to have you, but you must master it." (Genesis 4:6–7, NIV)

Then there is David, who at one point in his life committed adultery and was depressed until he confessed his sin. In Psalm 32:3–4, he described what it was like:

When I kept silent, my bones grew old
Through my groaning all the day long.
For day and night Your hand was heavy upon me;
My vitality was turned into the drought of summer.

But David did not stay down. In Psalms 31 and 32, we see him coming back to the Lord:

For I said in my haste,
"I am cut off from before Your eyes";
Nevertheless You heard the voice of my supplications
When I cried out to You.
Oh, love the Lord, all you His saints!
For the Lord preserves the faithful,
And fully repays the proud person.
Be of good courage,
And He shall strengthen your heart,
All you who hope in the Lord.

Blessed is he whose transgression is forgiven,
Whose sin is covered.

Blessed is the man to whom the Lord does not impute iniquity,

And in whose spirit there is no deceit. . . .

I acknowledged my sin to You,

And my iniquity I have not hidden.

I said, "I will confess my transgressions to the LORD,"

And You forgave the iniquity of my sin. (31:22—32:2, 5)

We have a beautiful example of David confessing this sin in Psalm 51:1–4:

Have mercy upon me, O God,

According to Your lovingkindness;

According to the multitude of Your tender mercies,

Blot out my transgressions.

Wash me thoroughly from my iniquity,

And cleanse me from my sin.

For I acknowledge my transgressions,

And my sin is always before me.

Against You, You only, have I sinned,

And done this evil in Your sight—

That You may be found just when You speak,

And blameless when You judge.

God has promised that there is a way out of sin, a way to be restored to Him. We see this in David's example, and it is clearly spelled out in 1 John 1:9—"If we confess our sins, He is faithful and just to forgive us our sins and to cleanse us from all unrighteousness."

What did David feel like after this restoration? He rejoiced in Psalm 139:13–18.

> For You formed my inward parts;
> You covered me in my mother's womb.
> I will praise You, for I am fearfully and wonderfully made;
> Marvelous are Your works,
> And that my soul knows very well.
> My frame was not hidden from You,
> When I was made in secret,
> And skillfully wrought in the lowest parts of the earth.
> Your eyes saw my substance, being yet unformed.
> And in Your book they all were written,
> The days fashioned for me,
> When as yet there were none of them.
> How precious also are Your thoughts to me, O God!
> How great is the sum of them!
> If I should count them, they would be more in number than the sand;
> When I awake, I am still with You.

Even when we are depressed because of something we have done wrong, there is a way out. We do not have to stay in that depression. Again, no matter what got you here, you are loved by a God of hope. Here are some more Scriptures that should be an encouragement to you.

Why are you cast down, O my soul?
And why are you disquieted within me?
Hope in God;
For I shall yet praise Him,
The help of my countenance and my God. (Psalm 43:5)

Trust in the LORD with all your heart,
  And lean not on your own understanding;
In all your ways acknowledge Him,
  And He shall direct your paths. (Proverbs 3:5–6)

Now may the God of hope fill you with all joy and peace in
believing, that you may abound in hope by the power of the
Holy Spirit. (Romans 15:13)

Rejoice in the Lord always. Again I will say, rejoice! Let your
gentleness be known to all men. The Lord is at hand. Be anxious
for nothing, but in everything by prayer and supplication, with
thanksgiving, let your requests be made known to God; and the
peace of God, which surpasses all understanding, will guard your
hearts and minds through Christ Jesus. Finally, brethren, whatever things are true, whatever things are noble, whatever things
are just, whatever things are pure, whatever things are lovely,
whatever things are of good report, if there is any virtue and
if there is anything praiseworthy—meditate on these things.
(Philippians 4:4–8)

Therefore humble yourselves under the mighty hand of
God, that He may exalt you in due time, casting all your
care upon Him, for He cares for you. (1 Peter 5:6–7)

I have been so comforted by some of these verses. One of my
favorites—the passage to read when you are really in a hole and it seems
completely dark and hopeless—is this:

We are hard pressed on every side, but not crushed; perplexed,
but not in despair; persecuted, but not abandoned; struck
down, but not destroyed . . . . Therefore we do not lose heart.
Though outwardly we are wasting away, yet inwardly we
are being renewed day by day. For our light and momentary
troubles are achieving for us an eternal glory that far outweighs
them all. So we fix our eyes not on what is seen, but on what
is unseen. For what is seen is temporary, but what is unseen is
eternal. (2 Corinthians 4:8–9, 16–18, NIV)

Your emotional distress could be coming from any number of
things. You have to find the source. Then you have to do something
about it. Often the hardest thing to do is just to remain faithful even in
the midst of your despair. Take a deep breath, and hold on to the Lord.
He will never leave you or forsake you. He will renew your strength.

But those who wait on the LORD
Shall renew their strength;

They shall mount up with wings like eagles,

They shall run and not be weary,

They shall walk and not faint. (Isaiah 40:31)

FIVE

Who Else Has Been Here?

A noble company of the anxious and obsessed

Tommy

One of the worst things about clinical depression and anxiety is that you lose all concept of time. When life is normal, you're used to the way a Monday feels, a Tuesday, and all the way through Sunday. You know how noon feels. You know how three o'clock, five o'clock, and seven all feel. You're used to looking forward to different events and anticipating their enjoyment. But in the middle of depression, you are aware only of now.

There is chronic and continual pain. Maybe not a physical pain, but one far worse. The sheer joy of being alive—God's common grace to man—quickly withers. The day creeps by in minute-by-minute increments that you have to endure. That was the way June and July slowly passed for me.

At times during the day, I would go over to our "barn," a two-story house for ministry, and go up to the top floor to lie on my face. There I would cry out from the depths of my heart. I found myself reviewing my life, wondering what I could possibly have done for God to bring this on me. I reviewed my theology and the messages I had preached, looking for anything I had said that might be incorrect.

Why? What reason might God have for putting me on the shelf? Week after week, my church would meet while I could not even leave the house. The elders and staff conferred without my guidance. Overseas, a conflict had erupted between Israel and the Hezbollah, and I felt my congregation deeply needed my perspective on it from the Bible—yet I was sidelined. Why?

Another maddening aspect is that I was hypersensitive to noise. My dog's barking, grandchildren's prattling, the phone's ringing—any sharp sound would irritate me to no end. There was a nest of birds outside our bedroom window, and they would begin their chirping at about five AM. I could not endure it. I had to get a ladder and dig the nest out of the gutter.

For some reason, when you're in this condition, you have no joy. A black cloud follows you; you observe all of life through a pair of dark glasses. Food is not tasty, nature is not pretty, flowers don't seem to smell, jokes are not funny, and relationships are cold. I remember one exception when my son John came home at Father's Day. John and

Ben, my two sons, are the funniest pair I know. When he was home, John made me laugh by doing a takeoff of a scene from *Singing in the Rain.* I remember the delicious feeling of laughing out loud after so long—it was wonderful.

I also found great comfort in something I had never quite appreciated. The congregation was told not to call me but to write letters to me. Each day, I would wait for the mail to come, like a kid at camp longing for a letter from home. And every day my mailbox would have five to ten letters of encouragement. Often the letters came from those who had been through depression and anxiety themselves, and my heart was greatly encouraged just to know that people had been through this and survived.

It is amazing what sense of fraternity I had with people who have walked this road. I must have received 200 letters. I opened them all, read them all, savored them all. Today I keep them in a bucket in my living room as a reminder of their encouragement. But I have never reread them because they bring up painful memories of my ordeal.

The day creeps by in minute-by-minute increments that you have to endure.

It's strange how perspective changes in a depression. I remember a professor in college who said that while serving in the Korean War, what he always reminisced about was sitting in a drugstore drinking water out of a glass with ice cubes. In all of the hellishness around him, that was the most pleasant back-home thought he had—ice water in the quiet of a drugstore booth.

My depression was much the same, making me look back on simple pleasures I could no longer enjoy. If I watched a basketball game on TV, I saw people cheering and laughing, and I thought how impossible it was for me to do that now. To me, the most wonderful thing in the world had been to go see my son play a game in Memphis, Tennessee, sit in the stands, eat a hot dog, drink a Dr Pepper, and sing "Take Me Out to the Ball Game." Now that just wasn't going to happen.

I found myself praying like George Bailey did in *It's a Wonderful Life*: "Please God, let me live again." For two months, the anxiety would continue but occasionally, momentarily subside. During those brief respites, I would devour the Bible and read until I could read no more. Inevitably the depression returned, and I would find myself resorting to incessant pacing. My body seemed to be on pure adrenaline, exhausted but too wired to rest.

One day the thought hit me—*I am Jacob Marley's ghost!* In *The Christmas Carol*, Marley's ghost wanders in weariness and constant agony, unable to rest between life and death. That's who I was. At the height of it, I understood how people could kill themselves. When you are in this chronic state that robs you of your life and all your joy, you think there is no hope, so death looks good. When your leg or arm or eyes or anything else goes bad, you do your best to work around it and keep going. But when the problem is your mind—your very means of perception—everything stops. Your life has ended until your mind gets fixed.

At this point, I realized the great dilemma a Christian faces with this problem. Try as you may to quote Bible verses on anxiousness, your body simply will not respond. You may as well tell a quadriplegic to work through the numbness or say to him, "When the going gets tough, the tough get going." Something more is wrong with a depressed person than one's will and attitude, but it can't be detected with an MRI or a blood test.

Luckily, no one came to me with the theology of Job's friends—"If there's something wrong with you, it must be the result of sin." I could now understand Job's response: "Miserable comforters are you all!" (Job 16:2, NIV).

It may have been a nonmedical thing that got you into the problem—poor scheduling, fear, traumatic events, overwork, or the stress of sin and its results. But by the time anxiety and clinical depression hit, you need help relieving the physical symptoms. You simply cannot tread water at the bottom of the ocean. Someone or something had better give you a hand, because mere exhortation will accomplish nothing.

My wife and I finally made a resolve. If something did not change quickly in my physical state, I was going to find the best doctor I could find to get thoroughly checked out.

Nothing changed. So I called a close friend on the Baylor Medical Board and asked him the name of the best doctor he knew. The doctor was a fine internist who was also a deacon at First Baptist Dallas.

After the doctor put me through a battery of tests, he gave me his evaluation. "There is nothing physically wrong with you. You have gone through classic anxiety and panic attacks." That was what I knew to be true deep within me but did not want to admit. *Anxiety*—something for the weak. "You might," he suggested, "sit down with a counselor or find a Christian psychiatrist."

I was the man who had just finished addressing an association of Christian counselors. I had written books on marriage and success in life. I had even written a book giving an entire overview of the Bible, and yet here I was needing someone to counsel *me*.

It was the lowest point in my life. Would I come out of this? Was *this* the "nervous breakdown" I had always heard about? Was I going to be an invalid? Would I continue downward and go insane? Would I have to be shepherded by my wife? Would I enjoy my family ever again? Would my church take care of me? Was all that I had striven for finished?

Steve

All the time I catch myself thinking things that are completely irrational. If you really pay attention to what is going on in your mind, it might scare you.

Just this morning I got a call from my dad, who is a worrier like me. We visited for a minute and then he said, "Oh, by the way, I am going in for a heart cath this morning. They may put in a stent. I have a 70 percent blockage in a vein. I'm sure I will be fine but just wanted to let you know so you can be praying."

Of course, I was very concerned about my dad, but my obsessive mind automatically went straight to myself. I started thinking about my own health—how I'd better take care of my heart, check my cholesterol, go see the heart doctor, and on and on. Once I realized what I was doing, I quickly stopped it and calmed down, but I can stress out without even trying to. It frustrates me that I can be so self-focused at times, but at least now I catch myself and stop it.

The line of worriers didn't stop with me, either. My fourteen-year-old son has just begun to worry about his health, but I am on it. We hold nightly counseling sessions in which I try to train him out of obsessive thinking and worry. For what it's worth, I do think a lot of genetics play a part here. He was born this way to some degree. But kids also pick up the habits of their parents, so he learns some by sensing his father's stress.

My ten-year-old son also has some compulsive thinking. He has recently started confessing every little sin. His mind races about the sins he commits, and he has to confess them to get relief. We are teaching him that he is forgiven already because he is saved by Christ and that confession to God is what brings restoration. We want him to confess to us when he makes mistakes, but not every little thing.

Both boys must learn how to get relief without having to rely on Mom and Dad all the time. We as adults can be the same way. It takes practice, but you can learn how to work out things between you and God.

So what is your story?

Does this sound like you? Your mind is racing. An all-consuming worry or guilt is so heavy within you, on you, and around you, you feel as though a gruesome monster is attacking your heart, mind, and spirit.

It's a secret battle. The load is too heavy to carry, but you don't know any way out.

You could never tell anyone what you are thinking right now. The thoughts are too graphic, too vile, or so embarrassing that you fear someone would laugh in your face if you shared them. Your thoughts could be of hurting someone, of deviant sexual behavior, or worse. If people knew the thoughts in your head, they might judge you to be the worst person on earth.

Even the people who love you most would shudder in disbelief and ask, "How you could ever think such a thing?" Surely they would look at you differently if they knew the real you or the you that is in your head.

Maybe you have done something that you are sure is a sin. You worry that you have disappointed God. You keep condemning yourself because you feel you need to pay a price for what you have done. Did you cheat on that exam ten years ago? Did you hurt someone, and you need to make it right? Is there some sin you have forgotten about that you are sure you need to recall in order to fix it? Do you worry that you might actually do that horrible thing you've been thinking about?

There is always something you can fixate on, and if you get closure on one thing, you tend to move right on to another.

Just this evening while working at my desk, I have had four clients with obsessive-compulsive disorder (OCD) call my cell phone wanting help with their particular obsession of the day. One client has called almost ten times, convinced that he must be gay. There is no evidence of this, but only of obsession and doubt. I want him, like you, to learn how to allow the Lord to heal his mind.

The goal is to learn to train your mind with God's help. When you learn how to delay the compulsive gratification of some obsession, you can begin to have victory. You'll learn that your world will not end if you don't do whatever it is you think you must do, say, or resolve. It feels bad inside for a little while, but you are going to get better at it with time.

Are you having trouble sleeping? Night after night you fight uncontrolled thoughts. If your mind could just rest, your body could too. When was the last time you had a good night's sleep? Days, months . . . maybe even years? If only you could switch off your brain, but you can't. Maybe you have turned to alcohol or another diversion to cover up the pain. It's nothing less than torture. But it's all you know.

The goal is to learn to train your mind with God's help.

You might even be convinced you are dying. All the symptoms seem to be there. Something does not feel right. You've looked it up on the Internet; you know it has to be true. It's going to be horrible. You don't want to die. You are too young; too many people need you. You just can't stop thinking about it or calm your heart. You wish you knew for sure whether you are dying, but you're too scared to find out.

Maybe you have a long list of personal rules you follow. The rules sound crazy. You have to wash your hands for so many minutes. You count steps. You are extremely worried about dirt and germs. You allow yourself to eat only certain things, or if you eat something outside of that, you have to pay a price for it. You have developed your own personal mountain of guilt.

Or maybe you worry about safety. Did you lock the door? You checked the locks, but you need to check them again. Someone may try to break in while you are in bed. Is the oven off? Did you turn the alarm on or off? The weather looks ominous. Those blasted tornados. Why did you ever move to a place that has tornados? Or, in your case, maybe hurricanes or earthquakes?

You may find comfort in strange things. You have to turn on the light just the right way, or close the door just the right way. You need to touch your favorite chair when you get home. You have to recite certain sayings to yourself over and over. The comfort lasts only a little while, but some comfort is better than none at all.

None of this makes sense to you. You are a Christian and have gone to church for a long time. Every Sunday you may think, *If I just act more like Jesus, then this pain will go away.* But it doesn't. Monday morning finds you struggling more than ever.

These are common stories I hear every week in my practice. In addition, many great men and women of faith have struggled in the past. We know that David was often depressed, overwhelmed, and hopeless. The apostle Paul said he would rather be with God than here on earth.

We find in 1 Kings 19 that Elijah was depressed and even asked God to kill him. Elijah felt he was the only one hurting. He had not seen fruit from his ministry, he was physically tired, he was comparing himself to others, and he had been on an emotional roller coaster. These all came together in a perfect storm to drown him in hopeless depression. Interestingly enough, in Elijah's darkest hour, God ministered to him with comfort and food. God may not bring you physical food, but He will certainly be ready to comfort you if you wish to receive it.

Martin Luther struggled with OCD as well. He obsessed so much over his sins that he spent hours in confession. He said he had hundreds of wicked thoughts per day. He was also so depressed at one point that he couldn't get out of bed. His wife came to him wearing black, and he asked her what was wrong, to which she replied, "God is dead." He screamed, "Woman, you speak blasphemy!" To which his clever wife replied, "Then stop acting like He is dead!"

The preacher Charles Spurgeon struggled with depression, as did John Wesley, who also had OCD and obsessed over his salvation. John Bunyan struggled with OCD and said, "Sometimes I have 300 blasphemous thoughts in one day." James Dobson tells of his own father, a faithful minister, who struggled with depression. As you've read in this book, Tommy Nelson, my own mentor and a nationally respected speaker, has struggled with depression and anxiety.

Some other people who struggled with emotional distress (according to their own admission, or from their stories) include

Ansel Adams

John Adams

Barbara Bush

Frederic Chopin

Winston Churchill

Grover Cleveland

Calvin Coolidge

Charles Darwin

Princess Diana

Charles Dickens

Emily Dickinson

Queen Elizabeth II

Betty Ford

Ernest Hemingway

Andrew Jackson

Thomas Jefferson

Lyndon B. Johnson

Abraham Lincoln

Michelangelo

Claude Monet

Isaac Newton

Mark Twain

Vincent Van Gogh

Rick Warren

George Washington

Clearly you are not alone! If you struggle with depression and anxiety, you are in good company. But what can you do about it? Where do you begin? First, besides identifying how you got here, you must accept your situation and turn it over to God.

By the time a guy named Matt had finished telling me his story, it had become clear that he was depressed and anxious. "What if my business doesn't pick up?" "What if my dad's heart condition doesn't improve?" "What if I mess up my kids with my poor parenting?" "What if I am not really saved?" The what-if syndrome had set in, and he was under its spell. He needed hope that can come only from truth. I told him, "Okay, what if . . . " The truth is that Matt was going to have to accept the worst-case scenario and trust God with it if he ever wanted to be free.

Next, to begin the healing process, you need to address three key areas:

1. Your mind—what are you believing about yourself, God, and others?
2. Your body—what is happening physiologically inside you?
3. Your spirit—what are you trusting in?

All three areas are critical to your emotional and mental health. As humans we tend to focus on the exterior. You may look great on the outside; it may appear as though you have the picture-perfect family and resemble the Waltons on a Sunday picnic, yet you know differently. You may be dying inside. Inside is where real healing takes place, and inside is where we begin.

What's Going On in My Mind?

I can't stop obsessing about it!

Steve

Allison feels as though she is a prisoner of her mind. Every second of her day is consumed by fearful thoughts. Her main obsession is germs. Most of her time is spent avoiding them or getting them off of her body. After touching anything, she goes through a ritual of washing and drying. Nothing is germ-free, and every object is a potentially life-threatening source of hazardous waste. Every room is dirty, every door knob is contaminated, and every wisp of air carries bacteria.

To make matters worse, Allison is filled with doubt. *Did I shut off the iron, stove, and light? I have to keep opening and shutting the door until the air is just right on both sides or it sounds just right. I have to start up the stairs with my right foot and end with my left, or else start over. The microwave must be set on an even number or the food won't taste right.*

Allison is not alone. You may even identify with some of these OCD behaviors. The interesting thing is that if you met Allison, you would think she is a completely normal individual. She has lived with OCD so long that she covers up all her compulsions.

What's going on in *your* head? It's a great question. If your thoughts and thinking processes are causing you pain, then you need to understand why and what can be done about it. A long, detailed lesson in biology isn't necessary. But understanding a little of how you were magnificently created and how your body was intended to work can help you make wise choices about some of the solutions that are out there for you. Let's look at the basic physiological part of what we need to heal.

Our brains are like highways of information. Inside our heads are millions and millions of roads linked to one another. Everything from our mood to communication to heart rate is being controlled there. Inside the brain are certain chemicals called neurotransmitters. These chemicals are like taxis that transport information from one place to the next.

They are transporting important information, such as:

"You should feel happy about . . ."

"That was so nice of her to . . ."

"What an incredible day this is."

"God is so gracious because . . ."

"Relax and calm down."

"You don't need to worry."

"Everything will be fine, just fine."

The taxis have a mission: *Let's get this message to Jill, because she needs it today.*

But these taxis also have mortal enemies trailing them. Certain enzymes are waiting like professional carjackers for the next taxi that comes along. When these enzymes attack a neurotransmitter, the good message it carries never reaches its destination. And the fewer neurotransmitters in your brain, the less chance you have of feeling good about life. In fact, if your brain does not get enough of the good chemicals for a prolonged period of time, you begin to experience depression, stress, anxiety, and fear.

Let's talk about your thought life for a minute. Like many people, you can be tortured by your thoughts. They take over and torment you until you become exhausted and hopeless. I believe most of this is based in obsessiveness. Obsession occurs when your mind stays intensely focused on a subject for an unhealthy amount of time. Usually, it leads you to irrational thoughts and beliefs.

Here's one definition of obsessiveness:

Compulsive preoccupation with a fixed idea or an unwanted feeling or emotion, often accompanied by symptoms of anxiety. A compulsive, often unreasonable idea or emotion.

This is where Satan's lies come in. Once you get to this place, Satan, the world, and your flesh take over and have a field day with your mind. This is why you have to work double time to keep your mind on the right stuff.

> Finally, brethren, whatever things are true, whatever things are noble, whatever things are just, whatever things are pure, whatever things are lovely, whatever things are of good report, if there is any virtue and if there is anything praiseworthy—meditate on [let your mind dwell on] these things. The things which you learned and received and heard and saw in me, these do, and the God of peace will be with you. (Philippians 4:8–9)

Many folks have thoughts that they would never tell anyone else— thoughts so graphic and horrific that they would be too disturbing for anyone else to handle. Then they begin to fear that they will act on these thoughts, even though they really don't want to. This is not uncommon. I have had clients share their deepest obsessions with me, and they range from the fear of killing their family, to having sex with their animals or children, to driving their car into an overpass beam or a train.

Some other common thoughts include seriously hurting yourself or others, sexual perversion, and your own graphic death. There are also thoughts about spiritual matters that can torment you. This ranges from the question of "Am I really saved?" to obsession over past sins, obsession over the possibility of future sins, and so on.

These thoughts are not from God and should be put out of our minds. Even though, as I said, the obsessor fears that he will act on these thoughts, in my experience he never does. The problem is that he spends inordinate amounts of time consumed with them and gets worn down.

Many people will pick one or two obsessions to fixate on. Over time their obsession will shift from one thing to another, but it seems that the obsessor always needs, desires, or seeks out something to obsess about. Possibly, this is because the overactive mind, left on its own, will always take a person to the darkest end of that road. The mind is such a powerful thing that the obsessor can have a long, drawn-out obsession in a matter of a few seconds. It can happen before the obsessor even realizes it's happening. It is very difficult to control.

You have to separate your obsession from reality.

Part of the solution is to recognize that it is just an obsession, and it does not define who you are or what you will become. You have to separate your obsession from reality and yourself. When you obsess, just call it obsession and identify it as such. It's not fact; it's not real; it's just obsession.

Yes, we must work at not having these thoughts by turning our minds away from them and sometimes by seeking appropriate medical help for OCD. But the fact is that if you are obsessive, you may always struggle with this, and it will consume you if you are not able to recognize the thoughts as obsession.

Most obsessors also struggle with legalism in their walk with God. They don't accept grace very well. I just talked to a young man yesterday who started by saying he thought he was depressed. When I talked to him about what his brain was doing and explained anxiety and obsession to him, he said, "I have never been able to put words to it, but that is what I do." He wasn't depressed at all. His obsessive thoughts were giving him anxiety, which led to feelings of hopelessness, which he interpreted as depression.

I had another client who was unwilling to ask his girlfriend to marry him because he feared that he might do something inappropriate with the children they would eventually have together. But he was not a pedophile. He had simply fixated on the worst thing he thought a human could do, and it had become an obsession. He struggled with legalism and obsessed about sin or guilt over sin. He was a perfectionist and extremely hard on himself. Most people like this have a hard time accepting God's love.

Is this you? If so, you need to understand God grace, mercy, and forgiveness. He sees you as beautiful and lovely no matter what obsession is going through your mind. Chuck Swindoll has a great book on grace called *Grace Awakening*. I highly recommend it.

How precious also are Your thoughts to me, O God!
How great is the sum of them!
If I should count them, they would be more in number than the sand;
When I awake, I am still with You. (Psalm 139:17–18)

Obsession can be a horrible thing to live with, and a huge number of us struggle with it. It leads to stress, phobias, worry, anxiety, and depression. We seek to train our minds away from it, and in the end many of us learn to live in a godly, peaceful way with it.

You can, too. Be hopeful and keep trusting God with your obsessions. Recognize them for what they are. Train your brain to move away from the lies and toward the truth.

And the peace of God, which surpasses all understanding,
will guard your hearts and minds through Christ Jesus.
(Philippians 4:7)

SEVEN

What's Going On in My Body?

I feel like I am dying!

Steve

By the time Stan came to see me, he had made numerous trips to the Mayo Clinic and spent over a year going to every doctor, specialist, and psychiatrist he could find, with no clues about what was making him sick. He had lost over $200,000 in medical expenses and had been diagnosed with fibromyalgia, chronic fatigue, possible blood sugar issues, potential thyroid deficiencies, many stomach problems, gastroesophageal reflux disease, high blood pressure, food allergies, and tachycardia (heart palpitations), to name a few. He was thirty-eight years old.

He sat down, told me his story, and begged me for help. I told him I thought he was suffering from anxiety, a little depression, and some obsessive thinking; then I taught him how to overcome those enemies. Within a month, most of his major physiological symptoms went away, and he began to feel much better. It has taken his body a long time to recover from years of stress, worry, and fear, but he is recovering.

I recommend that everyone get good medical help to address problems that doctors can deal with. So often, though, our physical bodies are responding to our emotional distress. Most folks who struggle with depression or anxiety have some physiological component with it.

Let's start with the effects of depression. Depression can leave you with very low energy and actually cause pain in your body. David spoke about this in the Bible:

> When I kept silent,
>   my bones wasted away
>   through my groaning all day long.
> For day and night
>   your hand was heavy upon me;
> my strength was sapped
>   as in the heat of summer.
> (Psalm 32:3–4, NIV)

People who are depressed often don't sleep very well. This is a vicious cycle. Your body needs a sufficient amount of sleep to produce enough serotonin. So if you don't sleep enough, you will lack serotonin, and that lack has the potential to worsen depression.

Depressed people tell me all the time that they don't need much sleep. I usually ask them how that is working out for them. The truth is that it is not working out so well.

You *have* to find a way to sleep. Your body is a machine that needs to be re-energized. The more you use up its resources, the more run down it feels.

Another characteristic of depression is that your mind lies to you about hope. You feel lost, alone, and hopeless. You may feel as though there is no use going on. This lie stems from the lack of feel-good chemicals in your body (not to mention that Satan loves this lie as well). The truth is that God is a God of hope, not hopelessness.

If you are a believer, you have cause for hope whether you feel like it or not. You have to put aside your feelings and run into the loving arms of God. Force yourself to accept the truth of God's hope, and don't stay stuck in the mud of hopelessness.

But as for me, I will hope continually,
    and will praise You yet more and more. (Psalm 71:14, NASB)

Now faith is the substance of things hoped for, the evidence of
things not seen. (Hebrews 11:1)

You need to have faith in something bigger than what you feel. Get outside of your emotions and grow firmly rooted in the truth of God's Word.

Trust in the LORD with all your heart

and do not lean on your own understanding.

In all your ways acknowledge Him,

and He will make your paths straight. (Proverbs 3:5–6, NASB)

All the time I have clients who come in depressed and have been diagnosed with chronic fatigue syndrome or fibromyalgia. Both conditions are physiologically very uncomfortable, even painful. Interestingly, in my experience, when we are able to make the depression go away, the other symptoms vanish as well.

Emotional distress just takes a toll on your body. High levels of adrenal release, raised cortisol levels, high blood pressure, the constant flooding of acid into your stomach, and the fluctuation of blood flow all contribute to the breakdown of your body. Emotional distress can cause all these things. If you fix the emotional distress, your body has a chance to function normally again.

Anxiety is somewhat different from depression. Anxiety manifests itself through two types of responses: mental and physical. Often people experience a mix of these symptoms.

Those who first sense mental anxiety demonstrate obsessiveness that leads to tremendous discomfort, almost pain, in their brain when the mind races and buzzes chaotically in every direction. They seem to be more of the true obsessive-compulsive type. Their brains just won't relax, constantly plaguing them without letting up.

The majority of anxious people, however, first become aware of physical symptoms. They often have something going on in their body, such as a headache, indigestion, bloating, backache, or sinus pressure, and that in turn triggers more anxiety. Yes, another vicious cycle!

If you have already had an anxiety attack with full-blown physical symptoms, the next time you feel some symptom, you start to fear that you are about to have another anxiety attack, which can actually trigger one. Sounds crazy, huh? But remember, you are *not* crazy, and you are not going crazy.

Just the other day I had a single young man sitting in my office who is a mature believer, works in ministry, and has everything in the world going for him. He didn't know why he was having chest pain, stomachaches, headaches, cloudy thinking, and a loss of motivation. As he described himself, it became clear that he was an obsessor who wrestled with anxiety attacks.

I have dealt with my own anxiety for almost twenty years now. Just yesterday I was sitting at my desk, and my lips and tongue began to tingle and turn numb. I immediately started getting sinus pressure, and my throat began to feel as though it was closing up. Ten years ago that would have been the start of an anxiety attack that could take me out of commission for the rest of the day. Now, I am able to stop the anticipatory anxiety and reason through what is going on.

Before, I would have automatically thought something horrible was happening to me and that I must be dying. Now, I stop and think two things. First, God is in control, and if I am dying, that is okay. Second, I focus on what might be causing my physical symptoms. In this case, the fact was that I had put antibacterial gel on my hands after going to the restroom and had rubbed my lips with my hand. After licking my lips, they all started going numb. I had begun to have an anxiety response, which caused my sinuses to swell (yes, that can happen) and my throat to feel tight.

I was able to recognize what was happening and reason my way out of it quickly. You can learn to do this too. It takes time and practice, but that's what I mean when I say you can overcome your anxiety with God's help. You are not a slave to it, and you can change.

Do not fear anxiety, or it will control you.

The mind is such an amazing organ, and it's so powerful. The more you can educate yourself about these issues and understand that you are not alone in them, the more power you'll have to overcome your anxiety.

Let me explain more about what is going on in your body when you are sensing anxiety. Remember that when you are having an anxiety attack and your body feels like you are dying, it is actually a physiological response to anxiety. You are afraid of dying, so your body responds physically.

First, your brain sends signals saying that you are in danger and should be afraid. In reality, you are not in any danger at all; it just feels like it. But now your brain is on alert. It tells your adrenal glands to release adrenaline for a fight-or-flight response, just as it would if you were in a real emergency.

But these are chemicals you don't need. Your body is being flooded with adrenaline, which is why your heart beats rapidly. Your lungs are trying to get more oxygen into your bloodstream, which is why it feels as though you can't breathe. Your stomach is releasing acid to flush out your gastrointestinal tract and shut down your stomach function, which is why you may feel nauseous and have diarrhea or acid reflux.

Your blood is being drawn out of your stomach lining, fingers, toes, and brain, which is why you may sense tingling in your fingers and toes and feel light-headed. Your mind is telling you that you need to either fight or run for your life. It screams that something is very wrong, and doom is imminent. These feelings are real, but they are not true. The truth is that you are going to be just fine.

Let's look at how to calm these fears. You begin by training yourself to believe the truth in these moments. Psalm 34 is a great road map. In verses 1–2 it says, "I will extol the LORD at all times. His praise will continually be on my lips. My soul will boast in the LORD; let the afflicted hear and rejoice" (NIV).

Are you afflicted? Sure you are—you are afflicted with fear. These verses were written just for you! The pain and fear are real. But this Scripture says to rejoice. But how can you do that? Your fears seem so overwhelming. You begin by praising God for all He has done so far in your life.

- You have taken the first step already and are seeking help with this book, and God is providing. Praise God!
- You have family and friends who deeply love and care about you. Praise God!

- You were there to watch your child take his or her first steps.
  How good is God!
- You looked outside and saw a magnificent sunset, and it's
  spring and the beautiful flowers are blooming. God is
  amazing!

Get the idea? You are doing what verse 3 says: "Glorify the LORD with me; let us exalt his name together" (NIV). You are taking time away from your fears to glorify God.

Here is something more to rejoice about. Verse 4 says, "I sought the LORD, and he answered me; he delivered me from all my fears" (NIV). God can deliver you from every single one of your fears. The truth is that this is just your anxiety, and it will pass. You don't have to fear it. Fearing it just opens the door for your anxiety to have power over you. You will gain power over your anxiety when you no longer fear it.

Another strategy is to adopt an attitude that says, "Bring it on!" Instead of fearing the anxiety, tell yourself, "Let's get this over with so I can go on." When you face your fear and believe that you are going to make it through, then your fears begin to fade. God designed your body to repair itself. Over time, you will find that what is a problem today can become manageable.

In the meantime, you may have to set some boundaries to protect yourself from situations that make you anxious. Like saying no to invitations, even when the person who invites you may not understand. You may have to skip that meeting or function to stay feeling safe. That is okay, but it is not okay to become a recluse. You should try occasionally to get outside your comfort zone so that your mind will discover you can survive it.

The bottom line is this: If you struggle with anxiety, most likely your body is paying a price. You have to learn to recognize when anxiety is happening and call it what it is. Your anxiety will be in control of you until, through the power of Christ and His truth, *you* take control of *it*.

Do not fear anxiety. You may feel like you are dying, but that is a lie. The truth is that according to Psalm 139, God has numbered your days, and nothing is going to change that. Learn to recognize anxiety, accept it, and live with it, but don't fear it.

EIGHT

What's Going On in My Spirit?

Deciding who is in control

Steve

Let me ask you a deep but direct question: Whom do you, _____
[put your name here], really trust in? Whom can you count on never to
let you down? Who has never hurt you intentionally? Who is the one
person you always turn to in times of trouble to help you figure things
out? If you step back and answer honestly, you will probably respond,
"Me. I am the only one I know I can trust."

Maybe others have so deeply wounded you that you have decided
never to let it happen again. Maybe you have pulled yourself up by your
bootstraps and survived some pretty terrible things by trusting yourself.
But you are hurting. In fact, you are dying within.

The stress and the anxious thoughts are eating away at you. Your need to control every situation has made you a twisted mess inside. Here is a question that I ask folks often: "You have done it your way, so how's that working out for you?" Honestly, how is your way working out? Probably not so good for many who are reading this book.

In my twenty years of counseling obsessive, anxious thinkers (and of being one myself), here is something I usually see. A root of fear determines the way we function, so we seek to organize and control the world around us. We manipulate people and our environment so we feel safe.

Think about how your world looks. Do you demand that your house appear a certain way? Do you insist that the people around you treat you with great care so that you'll feel loved? Does your desk or countertop have be organized just so? Must your children behave exactly as prescribed for you to feel comfortable?

I get bent out of shape whenever the shoes I left by the back door get moved. My world becomes uncomfortable when it does not stay the way I left it. The problem is that when you seek to control your own world and everyone in it, you become completely inflexible. You are selfishly seeking your own comfort and protection at the expense of others.

This is where the concept of letting go and letting God comes in. It is a lie to believe that you have control of anything. God is in control of everything. I have counseled many people who spent the majority of their time and effort just keeping all their ducks in a row. What a waste of effort if we are not truly in control! This is another form of perfectionism, which we will discuss more in the next chapter.

Although you may be successful in controlling some areas of your life, to have a healthy mind, you can't have twisted trust. *You* cannot be the primary focus of your trust, because *you* will run out of answers. The problems will become bigger than you and your limited ability to solve them.

To begin to really heal, you have to get to a place where you say, "I have come to the end of me. I cannot do this on my own. I do not have to understand, resolve, or have closure to everything. What I have tried to do has failed." The great news is that when you do that, you are actually moving toward biblical submission.

Proverbs 3:5–6 says: "Trust in the LORD with all your heart and *lean not on your own understanding;* in all your ways acknowledge him, and he will make your paths straight"(NIV, emphasis added).

You grasp the concept? It's not about you or how much you can understand or control a situation. It's about Him and His trustworthiness.

Now some of you may be thinking that you have tried various godly solutions. Maybe you've read your Bible for thirty days straight, joined a Bible study and prayer group, or both of these. Maybe you have tried stepping out of your comfort zone and shared your faith, or you have served others in some way. All of these efforts are honorable, but they do not solve your problem, because underneath you are trusting in your ability to work your way out of your pain.

You have to get to a place where you can allow God to heal your inmost parts. This means that the walls you have so carefully built to protect yourself are going to start coming down. Remember Psalm 127:1: "Unless the LORD builds the house, its builders labor in vain. Unless the LORD watches over a city, the watchmen stand guard in vain" (NIV). You have been trying to save your life and watch your own back. You are wearing out. Trusting in yourself sometimes works okay for finishing a project at the office. But it's terrible for finishing the work in your heart.

So ask yourself, *Am I ready to stop trying to heal myself so that my heavenly Father can do it for me?* Since you are so used to handling anxiety or depression on your own, this could very well be a daily battle for a season. At some point, though, you will realize how painful it is to try to carry this on your own shoulders and how peaceful it is to let Christ carry this for you.

We manipulate people and our environment so we feel safe.

Isaiah 53:5 contains the phrase "by his wounds we are healed" (NIV). Every time the men who arrested Jesus struck Him, Christ knew in His heart that it was for you. He knew it was the only path to real healing. He paid the price. Did He really suffer and die so that you could live such a troubled life? All you have to do is stop trying to fix yourself so you can exchange crutches for new legs—so that your spirit can rest.

A dear friend of mine, Buddy Vaughn, who has contributed greatly to this book, told me I could share this story from his experience:

The other day I got a call at the office from my dad around five o'clock. He said, "I just passed the road by your house. There are fourteen police cars at the end of your road. Some of the officers are standing with assault rifles. They are pulling a truck out of a ditch, and there is no one in it. I think the person they are after could be on your street. Call your wife, and tell her to lock the doors. Don't let the kids outside."

I thanked him, hung up the phone, and dialed my wife right away. My heart was racing. Every ring seemed to take an eternity. On the fourth ring, my eleven-year-old son, Luke, picked up. I spoke to him calmly but directly, "Luke, I want you to lock the front door and the back door and then get Mom on the phone." He could hear the tension in my voice.

"Dad, is something wrong?"

"Son, just make sure the doors are locked, and then let me talk to Mom. I'll tell you what is going on later."

"Okay," he responded.

My wife got on the phone, and I told her the situation. "I'm leaving the office now; I will be home in a few minutes."

It seemed the situation was even worse by the time I got there. More police cars were arriving. More guns were coming out. At dinner I explained the situation to my children. You could see their eyes widen and the fear build as they began to understand the reality that someone potentially very dangerous was roaming our little neighborhood.

At bedtime I called the police department. My children were

in our bedroom, afraid to go to their rooms alone. They wanted to hear the latest news.

"I'm sorry, sir, but we have not apprehended him yet," the female officer answered. "That is all I can say at the moment."

My kids looked at me. "Is he still on the loose?" they asked.

"I'm afraid so," I answered.

I could see my son begin to pace the floor. There was no way he was going to be able to sleep in his own bed. "I have two big windows in my room, Dad. I'll never get to sleep tonight."

"I have an idea," I said. "Why don't I sleep on the couch? That way I can watch the front door and the back door. You take my bed. That way you won't be alone."

"Thank you, Dad!" he said, and I hugged him as I sensed the relief come over his body. I began to get pillows for my night watch position, and my wife walked in to kiss him goodnight about ten minutes later.

"How is Luke doing?" I asked.

"Are you kidding?" She smiled. "He's already asleep. Without a care in the world."

Perfect peace comes from knowing that you are safe in your Father's care. Rest for your weary mind and heart comes when you let go of what you have been trusting in and rest in God's truths. You need protection. You need someone to watch over you. There are situations bigger than you that you were not meant to face alone. God knows you are scared, and He wants to take the fear away. He knows you feel alone in this, and He wants you to know He cares.

When you come to the end of yourself and can say, "This is too much for me," then God will be waiting to respond with "I have an idea that can help you be at peace tonight and for the rest of your life."

Give control over to God. It can be difficult to do, but it comes with the greatest freedom on earth.

keys to recovery

NINE

Escape the Performance Trap

Avoiding the poison of perfectionism

Steve

Have you seen the advertisement for Electrolux appliances, with Kelly Ripa from *LIVE! with Kelly*? It starts out with her waving goodbye to her TV audience and rushing home to cook a roast for a dinner party and some mac and cheese for the kids' sleepover. Then she simmers the chocolate sauce, tosses the dog his toy, hands out gummy bears, serves the apple juice at the perfect temperature, welcomes her friends at the dinner party, is the charming co-host, and then cleans the stemware perfectly as she ends the night looking for monsters under the bed. All in thirty seconds. Whew!

Another ad for a flashy new luxury car says, "Old success had warm milk and was in bed by nine PM. New success stays out and dances until two AM and can still be in the office by eight AM. Welcome to new success."

Judging from most of the advertising on TV and in magazines, the message we get bombarded with daily is loud and clear: *To receive acceptance and be a success, you must do, do, do and go, go, go.* Success at work, success at parenting, success at appearing the right way, driving the right car, living in the right neighborhood, getting the right flat-screen TV, having the right amount of cash in your retirement account . . . and on and on and on.

The world's message to us, everywhere we turn, is that we are what we achieve. Acceptance depends on our financial and physical attributes. We can have it all if we do it all, if we look the part, and if we become it all. If we perform well, we will live well.

But guess what. It's a lie.

Unfortunately, many times the church can send a message twice as poisonous. If it's wrapped in spirituality and mixed with some Bible verses, we bite harder into the lie. It's still perfectionism and performance, just dressed up in a religious package.

Often the drive for perfection comes from an unreachable standard that our parents imposed on us as children. Almost every adult I have seen for individual counseling came from a home where there was far more criticism than encouragement. Most grew up in a church that offered more damnation than grace.

One of the things that has helped me be healthy as an adult is that every day when I got home from school, my dear mother was waiting at the door to ask me twenty questions about my day and to tell me how great I was at whatever I had done that day. Overly critical, demanding parents will usually raise children who become perfectionist adults.

Do any of the following messages sound familiar?

- If you don't live up to Christian standards, God will not be pleased.
- If you are living right for God, then you will be blessed with good health and never have to worry about finances.
- Good Christians don't listen to anything but Christian music.
- Good Christians don't watch TV.
- Good Christians read their Bibles every day. If you don't, then you should feel guilty about it.
- Good Christians should be in church every time the doors open. If you are not there, then be prepared to hear the "We missed you, Brother, at . . ." speech.
- Good Christians never mess up—at least not in public.

The message we hear over and over is that to be a good Christian, you need to be involved in a certain number of Bible studies, outreach programs, Sunday school classes, discipleship training sessions, and so on.

Sometimes the messages are merely implied by well-meaning brothers and sisters. Other times they are preached loudly from the pulpit. Sometimes they are whispered quietly in the pews.

Fran and Garren were both firstborn children. They are now married to each other and have four kids. Both have successful jobs, and they are involved in church. Their yard is immaculate, their house is beautiful and clean, their kids all make As and excel in sports and the arts, and Fran and Garren are on task with their 401K retirement plan. But they are miserable. They are not doing enough, and they both hear their parents' voices in their heads, saying that they haven't put forward their best effort. They are failing.

The church can send a message twice as poisonous.

Guilt and shame for not meeting a certain standard come from five-point sermons, pointed fingers, and disappointed stares. No matter how it is communicated, the message is the same: *You are only as good as your performance. You can have God's best if you do it all, if you become it all. If you perform well, you will live well.* But it's still the same lie.

Here is some incredible news for those of us caught in the performance trap. If you have placed your faith in the saving grace of Jesus Christ to redeem you, forgive you, and restore you to a proper relationship with God, then there is *nothing* else you could ever do to make God more pleased with you or be more in love with you than He is right now.

Let that sink in. Performing Christian activities cannot make God love you any more deeply than He does right this moment. His love is not on a scale that tips in your favor when you are performing and tips against you when you are not. Do you know why? Because when God looks at you, He sees Jesus.

Romans 14:4 says, "Who are you to judge someone else's servant?

To his own master he stands or falls. And he will stand, for the Lord is able to make him stand" (NIV). God is the One who calls, redeems, and restores. He is the One who says that because of your faith in His Son, you are accepted.

Romans 3:21 says, "But now a righteousness from God, apart from law, has been made known, to which the Law and Prophets testify" (NIV). God had something better in store than the law and performance: amazing grace! Even the prophets knew something better was on the way.

Romans 3:22 says, "This righteousness from God comes through faith in Jesus Christ to all who believe" (NIV). Do you believe? Then you have righteousness straight from God.

Romans 3:23–24 says, "All have sinned . . . and are justified freely by his grace through the redemption that came by Christ Jesus" (NIV). You are justified, redeemed, and cleansed by Christ.

According to Romans 4.4–5, "Now when a man works, his wages are not credited to him as a gift, but as an obligation. However, to the man *who does not work* but trusts God who justifies the wicked, his faith is credited as righteousness" (NIV, emphasis added). You need to do the opposite of work when it comes to gaining righteousness. You have to trust that God is going to do the work of justification for you.

Now I can hear you thinking, *But what about James 2:26, which says, "For just as the body without the spirit is dead, so also faith without works is dead"* (NASB)? Excellent point. Let's look at it from Christ's perspective.

How can we tell the difference between when we are working to perform—to please other people or to be accepted in our circle of influence—and when God is working through us in the Spirit to produce fruit in our lives?

Jesus is clear. He says, "Take my yoke upon you and learn from me, for I am gentle and humble in heart, and you will find rest for your souls. For my yoke is easy and my burden is light" (Matthew 11:29-30, NIV). How weighted down is your heart? How heavy are your burdens? Are you finding rest for your soul?

If you are heavyhearted, laden with guilt for not measuring up, then you have not taken on the yoke of our loving Savior. You have taken on the yoke of performance and perfectionism.

Call it what it is, you have been caught in the trap. You bought the lie. Most of us have. It's dressed up in a neat package—pressure sealed, wrapped up, and delivered daily to us like our ever-growing inbox of e-mail.

The first step to breaking free is realizing that you are trapped. The second step is to look at your life and ask yourself the hard question. *What am I doing because I am concerned about what so-and-so would think if I didn't?* If that so-and-so is not Christ, and if the activity is not creating rest in your spirit and an ever-growing love for the Savior, then realize whose yoke you are wearing.

When you have taken up Christ's yoke, you will find rest for your soul. Say it out loud: "Rest for my soul." Doesn't that sound just like the abundant life Christ promised? Rest for your soul. And the burden? Guess what—it's light! Like the gentle, refreshing breeze on a spring day that warms you all over and reminds you that winter is over.

Then and only then will the fruit of the Spirit begin to grow in your life. Your life will become attractive to all those rushed and worried souls around you, because God will be able to use you and love them through you. You will have time to be patient, encourage others, and respond in ways only Christ would, because He will respond through you. Imagine the difference in your family, your relationships at work, your friends.

Don't take the bait for the lies any longer. The truth is so much sweeter. It has so much more nourishment for your spirit. We are going to help you get there.

TEN

Change Your Mind

Stop believing the lies

Steve

Last night, I spent two hours on the phone with a 48-year-old man. He had heard me on a national radio show and ordered my CD series on anxiety. He wanted to share with me his story.

He said, "I have hunted and fished all my life. I've been very active and have worked out regularly. But after a series of traumatic emotional events, I found myself barely able to lift my arms. I had extreme fatigue and no motivation to do anything. I have had tons of medical tests and all kinds of blood work done, resulting in speculations but no diagnosis.

"I really thought I was the only one who struggled with these symptoms until I heard your story. After listening to your CDs, I realize there are many who are almost exactly like me. Before hearing you,

I believed I was dying without hope of recovery. I now know what is causing my problems (anxiety and obsessiveness) and am able to believe truth and experience peace."

This is a phone call I get a couple of times every week, always from someone who is completely drowning in lies and fears without hope. It is amazing to see the healing power of hope. But hope comes from believing the truth that the Word of God offers. It is in such hope that peace, joy, rest, and contentment come.

This simple but revolutionary truth is crucial to your healing. To overcome the destructive forces that depression, anxiety, obsession, fear, and worry can have on your life, you must examine the lies you are possibly believing, identify them as lies, and get them out of your life.

It may sound basic, but it is profound. If you saw a caterpillar before it changed into a butterfly, you would never believe that a fat, fuzzy, wormlike insect moving slowly across the ground could ever learn to fly gracefully. But God knows what He created it to become. He designed metamorphosis so it could become a thing of beauty, literally a flying work of art.

We have to purposely retrain our thoughts.

We are not much different. We believe we are just fat, ugly creatures who will never grow beyond what we are now, when God knows He created us to be something else entirely. A lot of the time, we simply look at our circumstances and replay the negative messages in our heads that tell us we are failures, we don't measure up, we will never be good enough.

What we have to do is purposely retrain our thoughts to line up with what God has already said is true. You are what God says you are. You can accomplish what God says you can accomplish. You have the same spirit in you that raised Christ from the dead. This is the life-changing Holy Spirit who lets you talk one on one with the Creator of the universe, the Lover of your soul, the Alpha and Omega.

Meanwhile, Satan desires to destroy you with lies—lies from which, as Jesus said, the truth will set you free. Do you want to be free from the emotional distress that consumes you?

In John 8, we see the Pharisees accusing Christ much the same way that Satan accuses you. Satan uses lies and your emotions to convince you that you are not who God says you are. But Christ said, "So if the Son sets you free, you will be free indeed!" (verse 36, NIV).

Psalm 139 says that God thinks more precious thoughts of you than there are grains of sand on the beach. The truth is that if you have accepted Christ as your Savior, you are forgiven, pure, holy, and lovely before God.

Here are some common lies, each followed by what is really true:*

Lie: We are nothing but filthy rags because of our sin.

Truth: As children of God, we are forgiven and lovely before God.

---

* Some concepts adapted with permission from those outlined by The Therapon Institute with Dr. Paul Carlin and in *Who I Am in Christ* by Neil T. Anderson. Copyright 2001, Gospel Light/Regal Books, Ventura, CA 93003.

> If we confess our sins, he is faithful and just to forgive
> us our sins, and to cleanse us from all unrighteousness.
> (1 John 1:9, NASB)

Lie: You are defined by your past (the sins you have committed, the way you were raised, etc.)

Truth: You are who God says you are.

- You are the salt and light of the earth. Matthew 5:13–14
- You are God's child. John 1:12
- You are Christ's friend. John 15:15
- You have been chosen and appointed to bear fruit. John 15:16
- You are free from condemnation. Romans 8:1–2
- You cannot be separated from the love of God. Romans 8:35–39
- You are God's temple. 1 Corinthians 3:16
- You have been bought with a price; you belong to God. 1 Corinthians 6:19–20
- You have been adopted as God's child. Ephesians 1:5
- You are seated with Christ in the heavenly realm. Ephesians 2:6
- You are God's workmanship. Ephesians 2:10; Psalm 139
- You can approach God with freedom and confidence. Ephesians 3:12
- You can do all things through Christ who strengthens you. Philippians 4:13
- You have been redeemed and forgiven. Colossians 1:14

- You are complete in Christ. Colossians 2:10
- You can find grace and mercy in time of need. Hebrews 4:16
- You are born of God; the evil one cannot touch you. 1 John 5:18

Lie: The way you act tells you what to think or believe about yourself.
Truth: What you believe about yourself will shape how you act.

Lie: My needs are, and will continue to go, unfulfilled.
Truth: God promises to take care of all your needs.

> And my God will supply all your needs according to His riches in glory in Christ Jesus. (Philippians 4:19, NASB)

Lie: I can't help being full of fear.
Truth: God has not given you a spirit of fear.

> For God has not given us a spirit of fear, but of power and of love and of a sound mind. (2 Timothy 1:7)

Lie: I can't seem to escape my emotional turmoil.
Truth: You have the power through Christ to change.

> You, dear children, are from God and have overcome them [false spirits], because the one who is in you is greater than the one who is in the world. (1 John 4:4, NIV)

Lie: Depression and hopelessness are just part of my life.
Truth: God is a loving, kind, faithful, and compassionate God of hope.

> This I recall to my mind,
> Therefore I have hope.
> The LORD's lovingkindnesses indeed never cease,
> For His compassions never fail.
> They are new every morning;
> Great is Your faithfulness.
> "The LORD is my portion," says my soul,
> "Therefore I have hope in Him." (Lamentations 3:21–24, NASB)

Lie: God is doing nothing to help with my anxiety.
Truth: God *is* offering help with your anxiety.

> Therefore humble yourselves under the mighty hand of
> God, that He may exalt you at the proper time, casting all
> your anxiety on Him, because He cares for you. (1 Peter
> 5:6–7, NASB)

Lie: If I were a stronger Christian, I wouldn't have these problems.
Truth: Trials are what help a Christian become mature.

> Consider it all joy, my brethren, when you encounter vari-
> ous trials, knowing that the testing of your faith produces
> endurance. (James 1:2–3, NASB)

Lie: I don't deserve God's help.
Truth: You have been redeemed by Christ.

> Therefore there is now no condemnation for those who
> are in Christ Jesus. (Romans 8:1, NASB)

Lie: I am alone and without hope in my emotional distress.
Truth: As a Christian, you are never alone or hopeless.

> "I am with you always, even to the end of the age."
> (Matthew 28:20, NASB)

> "I will never desert you, nor will I ever forsake you."
> (Hebrews 13:5, NASB)

Lie: I am a victim of all the bad things that have happened to me.
Truth: We are victims only if we choose to be.

> And we know that God causes all things to work together
> for good to those who love God, to those who are called
> according to His purpose. (Romans 8:28, NASB)

Lie: I will never be content.
Truth: We can learn to be content in all circumstances.

> Not that I speak from want, for I have learned to be content
> in whatever circumstances I am. (Philippians 4:11, NASB)

Lie: I am a slave to my chaotic and confused thoughts and feelings.
Truth: God is a God of order and peace.

> Now we have received, not the spirit of the world, but the
> Spirit who is from God, so that we may know the things
> freely given to us by God. (1 Corinthians 2:12, NASB)

> For God is not a God of confusion [disorder] but of
> peace." (1 Corinthians 14:33, NASB)

Lie: I cannot overcome my problems and find peace.
Truth: Christ, the Prince of Peace, has overcome the world for us.

> "These things I have spoken to you, so that in Me you may
> have peace. In the world you have tribulation, but take cour-
> age; I have overcome the world." (John 16:33, NASB)

As you can see, there are many lies we can be tempted to believe. If we choose to believe them, it will affect how we live. The result will always be destructive. If we choose to believe truth, as Scripture says, we will be free indeed.

ELEVEN

Get Help from Loved Ones

How to involve others in your healing

Steve

After my wife passed away, for the first time I could remember, I found myself not wanting to be around people. I did not even want to be near my extended family. Remember that at this point I didn't know what was wrong with me; I just knew that my body felt as though it were dying. I felt very stressed, but I had lived with that my whole life and very intensely while my wife was sick and dying. It almost felt normal. I remember not wanting to make the six-hour drive home to be with my relatives that first Christmas. The thought of it made me anxious. I told them no, but without explanation.

All of my family had always gone to Nana's every Christmas. It was a beautiful time that everyone loved. So they just could not understand what they had done that made me not want to come up for Christmas.

The truth was that they had done nothing. It was me, but I didn't know why.

When I eventually learned what was going on with me, I was able to explain to my relatives how I was basically broken. I told them what would likely happen if I decided to come up for the holiday. The drive would stress me out. Then being away from my normal environment—one I could control—would be a nightmare for me. My anxiety level would continue to rise, and about the third day there I would feel weak, sick to my stomach, and light-headed. I would quickly come to dread contact with anybody. Then I would limp back home and spend the next two weeks straightening out my body again. It just wasn't worth it.

I didn't go home for the next two or three Christmases, but I had my family's blessing, because now they understood that I was suffering from anxiety.

We have resumed our holiday visits today, and we love it. I got better and you will, too. But for now, you may have to say no and learn how to tell the folks around you what is going on with you. It may be embarrassing to admit that you are weak, but that's reality, and you will be relieved not to have unneeded stress in dealing with those who love you.

Just this week I visited with a woman who had planned to kill herself. She had counted her pills to make sure she had enough to do the job; she'd decided where to do it and how she would be found. When I called her husband to talk about this, he was completely unaware of it. He wept like a child as I told him her plan. Now that he is informed, he has stepped up and begun helping her in her fight.

So often we struggle with anxiety and depression, but no one else knows what we are going through. We even get upset with loved ones when they don't understand. That is unfair to them and often our own fault. We must educate them. You have to figure out what is wrong with you and then find a way to put it into words so that they can begin to understand and see through your eyes.

First things first. You have to know what's wrong with you. You have probably read enough of this book to understand or have a general idea of what is going on. But you also have to learn not to feel guilty about your condition. Most Christians feel a sense of shame in being anxious, depressed, or obsessive. But unless these are caused by your own sin, you have no reason to be ashamed.

> *We get upset with loved ones when they don't understand.*

Some people think you are less of a Christian, or weak, or spiritually immature if you struggle with these things. Though none of this is true, Satan will try to use these notions against you to keep you from being honest with others about yourself. For years I always carried a "man purse," as my friends liked to call it. It was a backpack that I took everywhere just in case I needed anything in it—aspirin, decongestant, Xanax, Benadryl, etc. Remember, I was a hypochondriac, so I was comforted by having meds ready in case I didn't feel well.

My friends would poke fun at me, so I had to learn to be frank with them about my anxiety. In time they learned to tolerate my sometimes funky behavior. I know that it may be embarrassing to tell the truth, but you need to get over your pride and just be honest.

Obviously, you should use discernment in deciding whom to share with. Some people won't be able to handle the truth, but most, especially those who really care about you, will do fine. And it's always okay just to say you're not feeling well; you don't always need to say *why* you aren't feeling well. Sometimes you may have to cancel or reschedule appointments. If you just can't keep them, then don't. Avoid causing a crash in an effort to save face.

Once you know what's wrong with you and you're willing to communicate that to people around you, then you are ready to educate them. You're going to be fascinated at the number of people who will line up at your doorstep for help with their own anxiety or depression when they see you winning over yours. God just works that way.

> Because he himself suffered when he was tempted, he is able to help those who are being tempted. (Hebrews 2:18, NIV)

> [God] comforts us in all our troubles, so that we can comfort those in any trouble with the comfort we ourselves have received from God. . . . If we are distressed, it is for your comfort and salvation; if we are comforted, it is for your comfort, which produces in you patient endurance of the same sufferings we suffer. (2 Corinthians 1:4–6, NIV)

I see this so profoundly in my own experience. I am twice the counselor that I would have been had I not already gone through so much in my own life. Honestly, if I can help certain folks when few others can, it's because I've been there. You will be able to as well. Allow the possibility that God may be taking you through this so that you can, in turn, help others someday. It will happen—just wait and see.

To educate the people around you, you have to become a student of your emotional distress. Study up on it. Learn about it, and learn what you can do to fix it. This book will go a long way in helping you understand it. You have to inform the people around you, while realizing that they probably *won't* always understand. You will have to ask them to trust you with what they can't understand. Suggest websites, articles, and books for further information.

Once they get it, they will be a huge help, rather than part of the problem. Be patient with them. Think about how you were before you crashed and had to start learning what was wrong. I was completely intolerant of people who struggled emotionally before I went through what I did.

Pray for the people close to you, asking that they would have compassion. But avoid thinking you are special or more broken than others. You are not alone; many other people are going through the same trials.

You can have the support of others around you if you go about it the right way. You can't isolate yourself or push others away in anger. You must have patience with those who don't understand. If you do this, you will get more support and will get better much faster.

Tommy

A word needs to be spoken to the person who is living with someone going through anxiety or depression.

The first thing is to be a comfort to your loved ones who suffer. A good way to look at it is to be a safe house. Be the place of rest that they can come to. Don't tell them to suck it up. Don't tell them to be a man (or woman). Don't tell them to grow up. Don't tell them to get a grip. Don't tell them of the hardship they are bringing on the family. If your mate is ill, remember your promise to stay committed "for better for *worse*, for richer for poorer, *in sickness* and in health." I always knew that my home would be a comfort.

You may have to give guidance to your loved ones. They may not want to talk to another person who has been through depression, but they need to. They may feel that they should "white knuckle" it, but in fact they may need a doctor or psychiatrist. They also may need medication but feel that it is somehow a sign of weakness. You may need to be the voice of reason. Next, assure them of your continued, unconditional love. Let them know that you will still be there for them.

Be patient. This problem comes on slowly and usually goes away slowly, but it does go away. It's like a flooding river. The water recedes slowly, but it will recede. Meanwhile, make sure that you continue on with your life. You can be a comfort to someone without being destroyed by his or her crisis. Don't be disappointed at low points. Sometimes depression and anxiety go through a period called *looping*. This means that depression and anxiety can tend to revisit, although for a shorter period and to a lesser degree. It is almost as if the one going through it has a sensitive memory to certain emotions. So don't express your disappointment when brief relapses occur.

My wife was there with me through the hospital stays, the MRIs, the chest X-rays, the physical examinations, the panic attacks, the insomnia, the periods when I could not drive or tolerate loud noises or even family members. She was there when my indignation arose over the idea of taking medication and even being labeled with a "condition." If she had been part of my stress or, worst of all, took off on me, I don't know if I could have made it. Even in the times when I could not read or watch a TV show or sit still on a sofa for twenty-five seconds, she was there to comfort me. She could be stern when she had to be, but she was always a comfort.

Every person going through anxiety and depression needs an advocate like this. If your loved one doesn't have a spouse who is able to take on that role, offer yourself.

TWELVE

Set Boundaries

When to say, "It's not gonna happen!"

Steve

I had a phone conversation today with someone I have counseled for a long while. This man used to be successful and had crashed big time because of overcommitment. Within a year he was back on his feet and feeling great. The call today was the dreaded "I've crashed again" alarm. The problem? He had improved but then returned to the same frenetic pace as before. He hadn't protected his boundaries.

One of the biggest challenges for Christians with emotional distress is that they feel they can't say no. They sense that turning down a request is somehow weak or sinful or that it will lead others to think less of them. Although that could be true in certain situations, most of us who battle stress need to be able to say no more often.

God understands our struggles and gives extra grace when needed.

Christians think that doing more "spiritual stuff" makes for a more sanctified or successful Christian life. This is not true. Sometimes saying no to more church activities and yes to being quietly alone with God is what He desires.

At one point in my life, I was speaking two to three times a week, serving on an elder board, teaching a marriage and family Sunday school class of about 200 folks, counseling up to thirty sessions a week, and doing a daily call-in counseling show. Not to mention raising four kids and trying to be a godly husband! The truth is that on any given day, I have to work pretty hard to do even one of these well. So I'm sure you can guess the result of my overpacked schedule.

I started feeling very stressed and ready to crash. I did what I felt was the right thing—I dropped many of my speaking engagements, got off the elder board, let someone else teach the class, and cut back on my counseling schedule. It cost me financially, and the church didn't understand why I would not serve with my gifts. But I had to get past what they did not understand.

God's Word says that He will not give us more than we can handle, so if we can't handle all that is on our plate, then we need to evaluate what *we* put on our plate and what *God* put on our plate. Sometimes that means getting rid of what is not meant for us to do, even if doing it would help us look spiritual. God gives each of us a portion, just as Jesus described in the parable of the talents:

> "For the kingdom of heaven is like a man traveling to a far country, who called his own servants and delivered his goods to them. And

to one he gave five talents, to another two, and to another one, to each according to his own ability." (Matthew 25:14–15)

Some of us get five gallons of gas a day in our tank, and some of us get only one gallon. We have to be faithful with what He gives us and not try to perform like the person who has five gallons. Just be faithful with what He has given *you!* By the way, it is unlikely that you will have the same capacity in your tank that you used to have before struggling emotionally.

> ## We need to evaluate what we put on our plate.

Other things will also need to change if you are to get better. Besides setting boundaries on your activities, consider making changes in your diet, your media consumption, your friendships, your travel plans, your medications, your sleep habits, etc. You get the picture.

I had to make changes in all these areas. I could no longer watch high-action or deeply sad movies. Even as I write this evening, I am doing so because my wife wanted to watch a really intense movie about the holocaust. Too heavy for me today, so I chose to do something else. I don't take any type of stimulating medications. I can't drink coffee or sodas any longer. I have to get a good night's sleep, and you won't find me on an adrenaline-pumping roller coaster. If I feel that a sixteen-hour drive to a vacation spot is going to cause me anxiety, then I don't go.

Keep in mind some things you will need to push through and

make yourself do, like overcoming a fear of driving or flying or going to a restaurant on occasion. But don't be afraid to say no. Others may not understand, but you have to keep yourself healthy enough to be who God wants you to be.

A client recently asked me, "How do I know when I need to set a boundary and when I am just being selfish?" This is a difficult question, but the answer is that when you *can* do something, even though it may be a *little* tough, then pour yourself out and do it. But if it is going to cause you great stress, worry, anxiety, and depression, then make the decision to say no, and that is not selfish.

To sum up what biblical boundaries are, don't be afraid to say no, but be willing to push through a little so that you don't become paralyzed. You have to pray about this and find your own balance with God. You can do it. I know it can be scary either way, but you are a child of God, loved by God, and He gives you hope. He will not leave you or forsake you.

You will get better. He who began a good work in you will bring it to completion!

THIRTEEN

Let Medications Help

Where drugs fit in for a Christian

Tommy

Though a doctor had been giving counsel to me, I could not bring myself to act on it. I just continued day after day as Marley's ghost, drawn and quartered by this "thing" that had me in its jaws. I teetered on the brink of a netherworld. I could not go forward and reclaim my life, but I was not about to go to a hospital either. I spent each day pouring out my heart to God. I was like cracked and dry ground crying to heaven for rain and life. The answers would come from an unexpected place.

One of the most painful aspects of my malady was the strain on my wife. More than once I said, "Baby, I'm so sad that you have to go through this. You didn't sign on for this." Her reply was, "I said 'better or worse,' and this is one of the worsers." But at times her voice would crack when talking to her family on the phone, and I knew that it was out of sheer strain. Often a mate can compound the problem by an insensitive reaction. But I was blessed to have a wife and son who saw me as a casualty of being responsible. My wife never wavered.

No matter how vexed or angry I became, I could not shake the perfect storm around me. Sometimes it would show itself as a black pit of depression and other times as anxiety's maddening unrest. No gritting of my teeth, no sheer act of will could right my ship. I had wrestled with the Lord, and my hip was dislocated. All I could do was hang on to Him and say, "I will not turn You loose until You bless me."

A friend who is also my doctor called my wife one day, as he had many times, to ask how I was doing. But on this occasion, Teresa answered with desperation in her voice, "We've got to do *something*, because Tommy just cannot go on like he is."

Perhaps sensing that Teresa was near breaking, my friend sought advice from an Indian friend who was both a Hindu and a psychiatrist. The psychiatrist calmly seemed to suggest that there was something tangible, something *medical*, I could do. This was a turning point.

In retrospect, I was being exposed to two different worlds—the world of regular people and the world of the *experienced* who had been through or understood what I was going through. Those within that world understood what to do, while those on the outside just worked as best as they could with common sense and observation.

This Hindu psychiatrist was poles away from me theologically, but every day he dealt with what I had experienced only once in my 56 years. His calm response was, "Yes, Tommy has simple clinical anxiety and depression. He needs Ativan for short-term relief, and he needs Lexapro [an SSRI or a selective serotonin reuptake inhibitor] to build back his serotonin balance. The Lexapro will kick in after three to four weeks, and in the meantime, Ativan will take away the anxiety."

Something *was* clinically and empirically and scientifically and medically wrong with me. I knew it! And something could be done about it. Ativan has the effect of easing the "anxiety about anxiety," because you no longer fear it. You know you can take something to ease its effects, and it does not have control of you. An SSRI slowly lets your body build back serotonin, and you see the effects after about three weeks. He also prescribed Ativan as a sleep aid, instructing me how often to take a pill.

This is not intended as medical counsel that others should follow, because each person is different. But for me, this was the ticket. The psychiatrist felt that my case was pretty basic and "garden variety." My immediate concern was about developing a drug dependency, but he assured me that the dosage was low, short-term, and then only as needed, so I had nothing to be afraid of.

I felt as though I'd been in a boxing match against an overwhelming opponent and had finally discovered that he was indeed susceptible to a straight right. You throw it, you connect, and down he goes! You're elated, because you realize that your opponent is destructible after all. There's hope.

I began on Lexapro, and indeed there was no immediate effect. But about two weeks later, when Teresa and I were at a restaurant, I suddenly realized something—I was me again! For the first time since

May (it was now the end of July), the anxiety and depression had lifted. It was like having an intense toothache for which all of a sudden the novocaine takes effect. The clouds had parted, and the sun had broken through. A load had shifted off of me.

I looked at Teresa, and she looked at me. She said, "What's the matter?"

I said, "I'm me."

"What do you mean?" she asked.

"I'm me again. I'm normal. Whatever this stuff was, it has lifted. I'm me!"

In the following days, the anxiousness would go away and then re-visit, but it was not as strong as before. Whenever it subsided, it would stay away longer. The bottom line is that I had my life back, and I had hope. It was wonderful.

People in general and Christians (especially evangelicals) in particular need to understand something important. Anxiety/depression is a hybrid condition—it is spiritual, mental, emotional in its causes but physical and medical in its symptoms and manifestation. It must be treated with this understanding to be effective. If all you do is try to get at what *caused* the depression, then the treatment won't work. You might just as well exhort a diabetic not to be ill. On the other hand, if you merely administer medication and do not deal with what created the problem, then that treatment will also be lacking.

Two schools of counseling appear to me to specialize in or empha-size one part of the problem to the exclusion of the other. Christian counseling will deal with the overscheduling, the worry, the fear, or whatever else might have contributed to one's depression. But often Christians have a bias against doing anything medical. They feel guilty about having to take drugs for a problem that was caused by an emotional or spiritual crisis.

They need to realize that the medications are not some sort of "happy pills" but rather necessary tools for bringing one's body back to normal. They also need to realize that truly bad results can come from withholding medicine and trying to will oneself back to an equilibrium. The symptoms of depression and anxiety will linger, and the inability to live goes right along with it.

Christians have a bias against doing anything medical.

It's amazing how even some intellectually sharp Christians can all of a sudden become like members of an Appalachian "no doctor" sect in their aversion to medicine. I hate to say it, but I tell Christians going through depression and anxiety to beware of any Christian friends who don't actually understand the medical aspect of depression.

On the other hand, secular counseling will clinically treat the physical symptoms but often not deal adequately with the causes.

Both are essential. Pastors and Christian counselors should have at their disposal either an understanding doctor or a credible psychiatrist—both of whom can prescribe something to ease the symptoms and give a person hope so that he or she can begin to deal with the causes. A pastor should also have someone in his congregation who has *experienced* depression/anxiety so that the one suffering from it can have someone to talk to.

A fellow in my church named Carl had, years earlier, been through all I was now experiencing. When he came to me, he told me everything I was feeling, because he had been there. I would say to him, "Tell me I'm going to make it through this." Carl always answered, "You're gonna make it—I promise you."

I've heard it said that a person can go forty days without food, three days without water, three minutes without air, but only a few seconds without hope. "Abandon all hope" were the words that met Dante as he entered hell in the epic poem *Inferno*. Yet hope is exactly what you receive when someone who has successfully navigated depression is there to talk you through it.

Shortly after this point, my wife told me she wished I could visit with someone professionally. So I made an appointment with a Dallas psychiatrist. Now, a fundamentalist pastor visiting with a psychiatrist is a strange ideological meeting of minds. Yet as I sat down with this man, some years younger than I but accomplished in his field, it was comforting to see him nod in understanding as I described my symptoms.

He said that the appraisal of what was wrong with me—stress—was correct, and the path of dealing with it through Ativan and Lexapro was conservative and commonplace. He thought I might want to adjust the medication as I went along and hopefully wean myself off of it in about a year. Maybe 30 percent of those who start medication, he said, find that they feel much better staying on the medication. I have been able to call him frequently to get his opinion on some things, and he has proven to be a great help.

Steve

Early in my ministry and counseling career, I firmly held that believing truth, reading your Bible, and having enough faith were all you needed to overcome any emotional distress. That changed when my first wife passed away and I found myself in a deep hole of despair. I was reading my Bible daily and consistently. I was praying and involved in fellowship. I was using my gifts for the glory of God. I was trusting Him and being faithful to the truth of Scripture. I knew my Bible inside and out. I was doing all that I could spiritually, but it wasn't enough. I was still in the darkness of despair.

I have heard this story many times since then from some of the most faithful men and women of God I know. I came to the conclusion that my spiritual life was balanced and healthy, but my physical body was off. I truly believe that my body was just not doing what it was supposed to, and I had to get some help medically to correct what wasn't working. I began a journey of discovery about my body and what was going on inside of me.

I am not a doctor and in no way intend to give medical advice, but I can tell you what I did and what I have seen work for hundreds of other people. I didn't know what was wrong with my body, but I knew that my chest hurt all the time. I felt as though I couldn't breathe, my heart raced all the time, and my stomach hurt. I had chronic diarrhea. I felt dizzy and cloudy in my brain. My hands and feet tingled. I had unexplained sharp pains all over my body, and I had a sense that I was dying.

Now it doesn't take a rocket scientist to figure out that something wasn't right. What I found out from years of study is that my adrenal function was super high and my cortisol levels were probably through the roof. These were the results of stress and anxiety. I had always felt this way to a lesser degree, but I just didn't know what it was. It didn't matter what I did. Bible reading, prayer, breathing exercises, finding my happy place, exercise, belief therapy—nothing helped!

Once I accepted the fact that I was having anxiety and I couldn't change it, I gave in to the idea that medication was necessary. I needed something to correct in my body what I couldn't correct with my actions and beliefs. The medical folks will tell you that under high stress your serotonin has probably dropped out and your cortisol levels are likely high, so antidepressant and anti-anxiety medication is helpful.

I started taking Paxil on a consistent basis as an antidepressant and Xanax as needed for anxiety. I took Paxil for about six months, and to this day, I still carry Xanax with me for acute anxiety attacks, although I very rarely take it. After taking the Paxil for about six months, my anxiety level finally started to drop. But for me, Xanax was the most helpful. I am told that the anti-anxiety medication interrupts your brain circuits and stops the rapid fire of activity that is creating the anxiety.

If I felt anxiety coming on, I would take a small amount of the anti-anxiety medication, and within a half hour I had relief. It was so helpful to know that I had power over the anxiety, rather than feeling that it had power over me. One of the greatest fears among folks with anxiety is that an anxiety attack will recur. Knowing that I had medication to make an anxiety attack go away brought me tremendous peace.

You are not less of a Christian for trying medications.

Many mature Christians are resistant to using meds, and understandably so. I was, too. They feel that they are not being faithful enough, or that the church will look down on them as weak, or that God would not approve. Each person has to make his or her own decision about this, but there is no shame in accepting the Lord's help through medication.

Those who have not been through it tend to have a negative idea about taking meds. All I can say is that until you have gone through it, it is best to reserve judgment. Some of the people who have been most opposed to medical intervention have drastically changed their minds after dealing with anxiety and depression themselves.

If you are feeling depressed or anxious, doctors will often say that you have a serotonin deficiency. If that is the case, then you and the Lord will have to decide what is best. I do believe that psychiatric meds can be misused and overprescribed. Some people who rely on them need to deal more with their emotional and spiritual issues. But many others have done all they can and need to consider whether a medication can help as well.

Now the question comes up: What exactly does an antidepressant do? It is designed to allow your brain to create and keep the right balance of chemicals so that you can function the way God intended. These medications boost the existing serotonin that you have. When enzymes try to destroy the taxi (see chapter 6), the antidepressant intervenes to make sure that the message gets through.

Most of my depressed clients are prescribed an antidepressant (SSRI) and an anti-anxiety medication (benzodiazepines) like Xanax (alprazolam), Klonopin (clonazepam), or Ativan (lorazepam).

While I am generally against using drugs in place of spiritual health and healthy thinking, I do believe these medications are extremely helpful in the beginning. They can help get your head above water—especially a medication that gives you control over your anxiety.

So many Christians who don't understand it will simply say, "You need to just get over it." They mean well, but they don't understand the complexity of your problem. You have to take control of the situation and do what you must do to get past it.

Are antidepressants right for you? It depends. Some people don't need an antidepressant at all. They just need to retrain their thought patterns—or renew their mind, as the apostle Paul described it. Some people need an antidepressant for only a short time. Others need both a steady regimen of antidepressants and solid Bible-based Christian counseling to overcome their long-term struggle with depression. Be sure to try every resource available to you. As Woodrow Wilson said, "I not only use all the brains I have, but all I can borrow."

Proverbs 15:22 says, "Plans fail for lack of counsel, but with many advisers they succeed" (NIV). You want to succeed at this. Start with a

Christian counselor and your personal physician to determine what medicine is right for you. Antidepressants have several brand names, from Paxil to Lexapro to Celexa and many others. You'll need to have your doctor evaluate and prescribe them. Your physician, along with your counselor, will want to follow up with you from time to time to make sure they are working and are not causing unacceptable side effects.

If your general practitioner can't help, you may need to see a psychiatrist. A psychiatrist is trained in this field and can prescribe medications as well. He or she is knowledgeable about mental health issues from a medical point of view and can address and inform you the most.

Don't be afraid of medications. You are not less of a Christian for trying them. You are only giving your body the tools it needs to function with the right chemical balance as designed by God. Other things I have found to be helpful include sublingual B-12 vitamins; cortisol regulators; vitamin D3; fruits and vegetables; reduced sugar, caffeine, and alcohol; and getting plenty of sleep and exercise. If you want emotional stability, you will need to consider all these things.

Many people are suffering needlessly simply because they are ashamed to admit they may actually need medicine to heal mentally. It's a big step, no doubt. But it could be the right one for you. You are an amazing creation, loved by God. He has given counselors and physicians the ability to discover ways to help His children. Explore your options. Get a thorough physical exam and some good counsel. Then act on it and thank Him for it.

FOURTEEN

Live for the Long Haul

Taking preventive measures

Steve

"When will I get better?" I hear this question all the time from folks struggling with depression and anxiety. First, let me say that you *will* get better. I was so afraid that I was going crazy in the middle of my emotional distress. One day I looked up and realized that I had not had an anxiety attack for a whole week. Then a whole month, and so on.

I don't believe God will simply leave you where you are. But sometimes "better" is just learning to live with your emotional condition in a joyful way. More often it involves an easing of your distress to a manageable level. Let me also say that getting better rarely means returning to the place where you were before. Most people just want to feel "normal" again. They desire to turn back the clock and resume the life they once had. This just isn't going to happen. You won't ever be the same again.

Once you've been down the road to anxiety and depression, you will forever be a different person. But don't assume that this is a bad thing. Don't fear change. Now you can appreciate life more. You can be thankful for the little things. You can really enjoy feeling good instead of always taking it for granted.

You will need to retool and learn to think differently about everything. Your relationships will be different, but they can be better. Most things will be different; don't be afraid to venture into this new world. You might just find some really cool stuff. Giants will still be waiting for you and may scare the pants off you, but God is in the business of slaying giants, and you are now in the business of trusting God. That's a good combo.

Let me share with you the story of a man named Jay who used to tell me, "I am never going to get better," or "I'm afraid I am going crazy."

I sank into a dark, scary, lonely place around the end of May 2008. It deepened in the days that followed, until mid-June, when I could no longer work. I was crippled with anxiety and depression; I could not function in a normal way. I was overwhelmed by even the most trivial activities, including eating, showering, and watching TV. It was an extremely lonely place. I thought about death a lot and preferred it to living. I dreaded each new dawn; my favorite time of day was bedtime, since sleep was the only refuge I had from the depression and anxiety.

After I began seeing Steve, I turned to Jesus Christ and began reading the Bible daily. I can't say that it helped immediately, because it didn't. But the more I read, the closer I felt to Christ. He became my friend in my darkest hours.

My depression lasted for about ten weeks, though there was no single magical day when it all went away. My progress out of the depths of depression was gradual—aided by Jesus Christ, a compassionate Christian counselor, and medication.

I returned to work the Tuesday after Labor Day, thirty pounds lighter and still not completely out of the woods. Returning to work and the semblance of a normal schedule helped me get a little better each day. By Christmas, I believe I was about 85 percent healed.

I knew I was getting better when my interest in activities began to return, and I started not to feel overwhelmed by everything. It was slow—it did not happen overnight. But the darkness began to lift, and I felt myself coming back. Though I knew I was recovering, I was terrified that my progress would somehow stop. I did not want to go back where I had come from.

My entire attitude since then has changed; I will never be the same again. I am fully recovered now, but I have an awareness that I did not have before. And I have a relationship with Christ that I never had before. It's as if He sought me out, because for a few months to a year before my crash, I had begun to drift in His direction. I had a curiosity about Him and His teachings. I can't put my finger on it, but I was moving in His direction. I was being guided almost; I could feel it and sense it.

I don't think about the crash often. I know that prior to it, I had no idea that a human being could feel so badly and survive. I now know just how horrible life can be for one suffering from severe depression and anxiety. And that knowledge has made me a more empathetic, less judgmental person.

We need to discuss what life should look like after you are healthy again so you can maintain a healthy emotional disposition. Most people who have been through this are scared to death that they will return to the depths. That is unlikely. I never see folks go back to the way they were. You may have small setbacks, but rarely do people sink to the bottom again. This is because they know what got them there, so they do preventive maintenance.

It's important that you make adjustments to your life. You may always walk with a limp, but you will never be crippled again. If you want to have a consistently healthy emotional and spiritual life, start with two fundamentals.

1. *Spend time in the Word of God.* "All Scripture is inspired by God and profitable for teaching, for reproof, for correction, for training in righteousness" (2 Timothy 3:16, NASB). The more you read your Bible, the better you will know God. The better you know God, the more you will trust Him. The more you trust Him, the less fear, worry, stress, anxiety, and depression you will have. You also need to memorize Scripture. When you hide God's Word in your heart, it will flow out into your life.

2. *Develop a good prayer life.* Learn to pray thankfully. When you spend a majority of your prayer life thanking God for all things and

praising Him for the life you have, you will find yourself experiencing more joy, peace, contentment, rest, and hope.

Anxiety and depression look different when it comes to preventive maintenance. I will address both.

Anxiety—Many folks who think they are depressed are actually experiencing anxiety and stress, which result in feelings of hopelessness, which lead to the false conclusion that they are depressed. When you experience anxiety, something deep inside you convinces you that life is dangerously gloomy and hopeless. It is not even necessarily a conscious thought or feeling, but it is there.

Anxiety, stress, worry, and fear all fall into the same category. To manage them, you have to be willing to do some hard things. For the rest of your life, you will need to continue to train your mind away from stinkin' thinkin'. You have to continue to root out the lies that you believe and replace them with God's truth.

You won't ever be the same again.

Remember that one of the dangers you will face is what we call anticipatory anxiety. If you fear having anxiety, that may *cause* you to have anxiety. So you have to let go of that fear. Be willing always to accept worst-case scenarios. At some point, you just have to lay down your fears and give them all to God. You can do it. You have to be brave and courageous, but you can do it.

From here on, you need to manage your time wisely. This will probably mean cutting out some stressful things and carrying less responsibility. I follow a little routine that works wonderfully. When I sense that I am starting to get overwhelmed, I make a list of my stressors. I mean *all* of them, from paying the mortgage, to repairing the fence, to ministering to kids, to mowing the yard. Everything must be put on the table so that you and God can decide what to take off of it. Make the list, and divide it into two categories. Things you can change, and things you can't.

Things you can change—If you can change something and you feel God wants you to, then change it. Maybe it's paying someone to mow for you or clean your house. Or it's selling your house, getting a new job, and moving to another city. If it stresses you and you can change it while still being within the will of God, then go for it. Don't be afraid. You must have shallow roots and a loose grip: shallow roots for God to move you wherever He wants you to go, and a loose grip so you don't hold on to anything too tightly.

Trust me, God can pry your fingers off anything you are clinging to. He will have no other gods before Him. If you have something in your grip, He can, and often will, demonstrate His love for you by taking it away.

Things you can't change—If you can't change it, then you have to be willing to accept it and move on. Maybe it's a health problem or a spouse who doesn't love you well or an adult child who has gone astray. So many people stay bogged down with despair over things that are not in their control. You have to give these things to God, and you must allow Him to take care of them. Use the old Serenity Prayer, which goes like this:

God grant me the serenity
to accept the things I cannot change;
courage to change the things I can;
and wisdom to know the difference.

Living one day at a time,
Enjoying one moment at a time,
Accepting hardships as the pathway to peace;
Taking, as He did, this sinful world
as it is, not as I would have it;
Trusting that He will make all things right
if I surrender to His Will;
That I may be reasonably happy in this life
and supremely happy with Him
Forever in the next.
Amen.

—attributed to Reinhold Niebuhr

Surrendering to God will lead you to emotional freedom.

Depression—Now depression is a different story. Usually the people around you will notice you are better before you do. It is common for someone struggling with depression to one day look up and say, "I'm back" or "I'm me again."

There are many faces of depression, but the two I see most often are those who've had a long-term, fairly constant battle with it, and those who had more of a sudden onset. Those with a long, drawn-out battle will often climb out more slowly, while those who came into it quickly will emerge from it quickly as well.

People who have fought and overcome depression are also afraid they will return to it. But like anxiety, knowing the reasons you got there—often depleting yourself emotionally, physically, and/or spiritually—gives you a strong chance of avoiding those pitfalls again. So keep a journal to help identify circumstances that negatively affect your outlook or behavior.

Some of the things you have to do to maintain emotional stability after depression are simply common sense that you have heard before. You have to get good sleep. That means six to eight hours a night. You need a good diet and plenty of exercise. You also have to work on your thought life; you must dwell on the right stuff.

> Finally, brethren, whatever things are true, whatever things are noble, whatever things are just, whatever things are pure, whatever things are lovely, whatever things are of good report, if there is any virtue and if there is anything praiseworthy—meditate on these things. (Philippians 4:8)

If you *believe* that life is dreary and hopeless, you will *feel* that way. On the other hand, an optimistic, joyful, hopeful thought life will produce those kinds of feelings. This is not easy for someone who may have spent most of his or her life thinking the other way, but with some brain training, you can master it. Believe the truth about who you are in Christ, and the truth will set you free.

Walking on Water

Seven steps to joy, rest, contentment, and hope

Tommy

In the depths of my depression, I would sometimes go to the top floor of our barn and preach to myself. I took Ephesians 1 and preached it just to feel the joy of the Holy Spirit in the proclamation of the Word. The thought of once again standing in the pulpit was like a light at the end of the tunnel.

There were times when I would stop at the church instead of driving by, walk into the empty sanctuary, and stand at the pulpit. I would run my hands along the smooth edges of the "sacred desk" and let my eyes move about, imagining where the familiar faces would be.

It took about two months before I finally got a medication that relieved my symptoms, and then it took about a month to gain my life back.

Meanwhile, I was making preparations to get back in the pulpit. I scheduled various Bible studies for just a dozen or so people to get my feet wet and to find out if I could teach with the same energy. I could, and it was marvelous.

I also found out how wonderful it was just to enjoy simple things I had taken for granted in the past:

To sit and delight in feeling normal

To read and absorb knowledge

To enjoy the human warmth of family and friends at a meal

To lie in my bed and read until I became sleepy, and then turn off the light and fall into a natural and pleasant sleep.

You realize that the most wonderful thing about life *is* life. There is joy simply in being alive. In a depression, you do not feel any of life's joy. But once you are restored, all you really need is to breathe.

Still, I looked forward to preaching again. I had to call off most of what I had put on hold earlier—the Song of Solomon conferences, the Young Guns program, traveling to speak, and two of my men's Bible studies. But the pulpit still remained prominent in my mind.

My first Sunday back, I shared with the congregation for about ten minutes on what I had been through. Though Christians may not want to talk about depression, as a pastor who had disappeared for four months, I did not have the privilege of concealing where I'd been.

I didn't receive even one discouraging or judgmental word. Rather, I received a stack of letters and e-mails from people in the congregation who had been through exactly what I had been through, but no one knew. I found out that two of my elders, three of my staff, and my secretary had gone through clinical depression.

As my message went out on tape or CD, I began receiving calls from people all over the country who were going through depression and wanted advice. As a matter of fact, I went from being the guy who spoke about the Song of Solomon and sex to the "depression guy." I learned to value others' sympathy as each day my mailbox was filled with letters and prayers. Christ's body drew around its fallen.

There is joy simply in being alive.

I found out that when your perception of reality is flawed and all you can do is pray, suffer, and wait, then you learn about the grace of God. Sometimes people who go through depression appear to experience a strange sort of baptism—a baptism of fire and purification, one that comes from not being able even to lift the shield of faith but just lying weary beneath it. Depression will draw you into a breath-by-breath relationship with God.

In fact, a number of good things can come from this affliction.

For one, as I mentioned before, you learn to delight in just feeling normal and good. "It is good for the eyes to see the sun" (Ecclesiastes 11:7, NASB). Being alive is a delight that you can take for granted—until it is taken away. You learn to thank God for being normal.

Next, you learn to appreciate the Bible. A depression or anxiety can take away your ability to emotionally engage the Word of God. This was the greatest of distresses during my affliction—I could not read my Bible for any length of time. Never again will I take for granted simply reading and delighting in the Word of God. What joy it is to soak in the Scriptures! In my recovery, I began to read not just for sermon preparation but for the pure joy of learning. The delight of "the books" (2 Timothy 4:13) had come back.

Another blessing I got from going through depression is that I learned to empathize. Never again will I look at those who are struggling with depression or anxiety in the way I had looked at them before. The tendency is to see them as weak. But once you experience the clinical nature of depression or anxiety, you are forever quick to come to their aid. That is why you are initially desperate to find someone who has been through depression and can guide you through it from first-hand experience. You need to know from a survivor that there is hope.

I found a deeper appreciation of my wife's love. I found out that a great many marriages break up over depression, because the mate simply can't get a handle on what his or her spouse is experiencing. I truly don't know what I would have done without Teresa, because we went through it as a couple. I've also learned to listen to her counsel with a more attentive ear when she says I'm overloading. Teresa was with me through it all.

In short, as Dickens wrote in *A Tale of Two Cities,* "It was the best of times, it was the worst of times." I wouldn't repeat what I went through for anything, but I would not trade the experiences either. I discovered in a new way "the breadth and length and height and depth, and to know the love of Christ which surpasses knowledge." (Ephesians 3:18–19, NASB). I realized that when I was in a dark wilderness with no concept of what God was doing, His lovingkindness and truth followed me all my days. I realized, like Joseph of old, that God had plans that transcended all my senses, and I could learn to rest in Him.

I know there will come a day when other pains will befall me, and someday I'll hear the inevitable command to "get your affairs in order." But I will navigate that day, because I have been to the bottom of the sea and He was there. As Corrie ten Boom said, "There is no pit so deep that God's love is not deeper still."

Psalm 84:6 says, "As they pass through the Valley of Baca, they make it a place of springs"(NIV). *Baca* means weeping. When we go through times of weeping, we are only passing through. But God will turn the pain into a place of blessing for all who go that way. Our pain can become a future blessing to others.

Steve

In summary, here are seven steps from the book of Philippians that you can take to start healing from the emotional pain of anxiety and depression.

1. *Don't stay stuck in the past or become a victim of your past.* God is a God of future hope, not a God of a painful past.

> Brethren, I do not count myself to have apprehended; but one thing I do, forgetting those things which are behind and reaching forward to those things which are ahead. (Philippians 3:13)

2. *Stay focused on Christ and not on yourself.* Turning in on yourself leads to misery. Turning outward leads to blessing others and God.

I press toward the goal for the prize of the upward call of God in Christ Jesus. (Philippians 3:14)

3. *Learn to rejoice always in all things.*

Rejoice in the Lord always. Again I will say, rejoice! (Philippians. 4:4)

4. *Remember that fear is not from God.* We must learn to be thankful for everything God allows to happen in our lives—even the hard times. Prayer, trust, and gratitude will produce a peace that keeps our minds safe in Christ.

Be anxious for nothing, but in everything by prayer and supplication, with thanksgiving, let your requests be made known to God; and the peace of God, which surpasses all understanding, will guard your hearts and minds through Christ Jesus. (Philippians 4:6–7)

5. *Get rid of your stinkin' thinkin'.* Satan is the father of lies and desires to destroy you with them. God is a God of truth, and Scripture says that the truth will set you free. If you stay focused on what is wrong with your life and believe lies about yourself and God, you will have

no peace, joy, or hope. On the other hand, if you dwell on the things of the Lord, as the apostle Paul said, the God of peace will be with you.

> Finally, brethren, whatever things are true, whatever things are noble, whatever things are just, whatever things are pure, whatever things are lovely, whatever things are of good report, if there is any virtue and if there is anything praiseworthy—meditate on these things. The things which you learned and received and heard and saw in me, these do, and the God of peace will be with you. (Philippians 4:8–9)

6. *Learn contentment through Christ.* This takes real effort. You literally have to train yourself to be content. The next time you are unsettled or discontent, stop and make yourself pray and refocus on Him.

> Not that I speak in regard to need, for I have learned in whatever state I am, to be content: I know how to be abased, and I know how to abound. Everywhere and in all things I have learned both to be full and to be hungry, both to abound and to suffer need. I can do all things through Christ who strengthens me. (Philippians 4:11–13)

7. *Know that God is sufficient for all your needs.* We think we need a lot of things, but Scripture says we really need only Him. Let His mercy, grace, and love be enough.

And my God shall supply all your need according to His riches in glory by Christ Jesus. (Philippians 4:19)

I have never been more joyful, peaceful, restful, and hopeful than I am today. I have been remarried for thirteen years now to Marty, a woman of God. We have four amazing children, and God has continued to use me and my story over and over in the lives of thousands.

No matter where you are today, you can have hope. Hope will come only through Christ and a total reliance on Him. My prayer for you is that God will use your experience fot His glory. Hang in there, keep holding on, and wait for God to bring you to a place of peace. The darkness that you may be experiencing now will not last forever. Things will get better. You *will* walk on water.

FOCUS ON THE FAMILY®

Welcome to the Family

Whether you purchased this book, borrowed it, or received it as a gift, thanks for reading it! This is just one of many insightful, biblically based resources that Focus on the Family produces for people in all stages of life.

Focus is a global Christian ministry dedicated to helping families thrive as they celebrate and cultivate God's design for marriage and experience the adventure of parenthood. Our outreach exists to support individuals and families in the joys and challenges they face, and to equip and empower them to be the best they can be.

Through our many media outlets, we offer help and hope, promote moral values and share the life-changing message of Jesus Christ with people around the world.

Focus on the Family MAGAZINES

These faith-building, character-developing publications address the interests, issues, concerns, and challenges faced by every member of your family from preschool through the senior years.

For More INFORMATION

 ONLINE:
Log on to
FocusOnTheFamily.com
In Canada, log on to
FocusOnTheFamily.ca

 PHONE:
Call toll-free:
**800-A-FAMILY
(232-6459)**
In Canada, call toll-free:
800-661-9800

THRIVING FAMILY®
Marriage & Parenting

**FOCUS ON
THE FAMILY
CLUBHOUSE JR.®**
Ages 4 to 8

**FOCUS ON
THE FAMILY
CLUBHOUSE®**
Ages 8 to 12

**FOCUS ON
THE FAMILY
CITIZEN®**
U.S. news issues

Rev. 3/11

More expert resources
for marriage and parenting . . .

Do you want to be a better parent? Enjoy a stronger marriage? Focus on the Family's collection of inspiring, practical resources can help your family grow closer and stronger than ever before. Whichever format you might need—video, audio, book or e-book, we have something for you. Visit our online Family Store and discover how we can help your family thrive at **FocusOnTheFamily.com/resources**.